INTREE

O'Sullevan's GRAND NATIONAL GUIDE

By Peter O
who gave a 13—2 a
including his sec
Royal Ascot nap.

set to jump ... the Kremlin!

combination in
t-ever, most inter-
onal will have to
ating the height of
g 4½ miles—or more
oscow's Red Square,
ic feature is the first
resented by seven-
winner of a steeple-
best Moscow-trained

Last night's call-over

GRAND NATIONAL
Run tomorrow. 4 miles 856 yards.

	March 16	March 20	last night
MERRYMAN II	10-1	10-1	8-1
JONJO	33-1	25-1	12-1
TEAM SPIRIT	16-1	14-1	14-1
HUNTER'S BREEZE	20-1	16-1	16-1
BADANLOCH	11-1	16-1	16-1
SIRACUSA	20-1	18-1	18-1
O'MALLEY POINT	25-1	20-1	18-1
CANNOBIE LEE	22-1	16-1	20-1
MR. WHAT	20-1	16-1	20-1
SCOTTISH FLIGHT II	25-1	20-1	20-1
OXO	20-1	18-1	25-1
KILMORE	33-1	33-1	33-1
NICOLAUS SILVER			33-1
WYNDBURGH	25-1	25-1	33-1
ERNEST			33-1
VIVANT			40-1
BANTRY BAY	40-1		40-1
CARRASCO			40-1
CLOVER BUD			40-1
FLOATER			40-1
IRISH COFFEE			40-1
JIMURU			40-1
KINGSTEL			40-1
TAXIDERMIST			50-1
TEA FIEND			50-1
WILY ORIENTAL			50-1
OSCAR WILDE		40-1	50-1
APRIL QUEEN			66-1
BRIAN OGE			100-1
DOUBLE CREST			100-1
FRESH WINDS			100-1
PENNY FEATHER			100-1
SABERIA			100-1
IMPOSANT			100-1

THE £5 M
qualificatio
what the
are calling
decision o
Ascot stewa
ing   ye
Coronation

With the s
33—1 outside
the duel in th
backers and l
swung heavily
favour.

Thousands o
odds-on favour
Million had lo
soned their ti
official inquiry

Its sequel—th
of the winner
punters competi
search for winnin

What happen
attention of rac
viewers alike w
the leading gro
the home turn
Buz Kashi, who

ish I had not

11/12/75

—Mrs. Topham

racing round
seeking "dayligh
challenge.

As One In A
the lead with le
to run the race
suddenly the y
colours of the "
upon the inside
a one-and-a-half

Film patrol
the stewards tha
sufficiently infrin
only to warrant d
to justify a four-
the rider, starting

P—
of
ng
the
on-
-old
ed:
uld
lise

any
say
not
her

the
with

nly
the
ase
ere
in

the
ng's
nale
'My
at

per-
I to
rse
the
Levy

By Peter O'Sullevan

7 naps in the last 8 and a 7—1 double yesterday

connection with the National
introduced a high element of
pre-race suspense, characterised
in 1952 by a dispute with the
B.B.C., which resulted in her
relaying her own not entirely
successful broadcast.

It was not until 1964 that
the first "death-bed" National
was decided—Mrs. Topham having proclaimed that the burden of upkeep was more than
a small family enterprise could
continue to underwrite.

Euphoric

The list of possible pur-
chasers of the site, acquired
by Topham's as lessees from
Lord Sefton for £275,000, is too
lengthy to catalogue.

In a euphoric atmosphere at
the Savoy on November 19 two
years ago. Mrs. Topham, who
was presented by the new
purchaser, Bill Davies with the
Grand National winning-post,
which is installed in the garden
of her Isle of Wight home was

Mirabel Topham
... ended her silence

National is safeguarded for
another five years at least."

To which Mr. D added:
"And I hope for my lifetime."

Next August, lively, voluble
and engagingly humorous
Mrs. T will be 85. "And my
dog, Captain Becher, will be
9½." she reflected yesterday,
when replying shortly to the
£3 million question: "Do you
regret having sold to Mr.
Davies?"—"I do."

Every year's neglect means
seven years work, she insisted
when stressing the need for
urgent action by the
authorities.

In the more immediate

change of plan for one of
England's most exciting young
jumping stars, Border Incident.
who was expected to forego
hurdling for 'chasing this
season.

"He's been off since March."
reflects the trainer of the
scintillating winner of all his
three outings in the '74-5
season, "and we think it's
about time he had an airing."

Even so, Border Incident's
bid for Saturday's S.G.B.
Hurdle at Ascot may be a
'one-off.'

His future campaign will be
deliberated after the event by
partner - owners, Anthony
Warrender (half - share) and
Alistair Hoyer-Miller and Lord
Sudley, who each own 'a leg.'

Another S.G.B. "probable"
who'll be determining his own
future programme by his perform

'T
pos
S.G.
ulti
dep
the

Th
the
peti
'po
miss

Exam   Brass (2.0,
nap), who should "collect"
this afternoon at Carlisle,
where Greystoke Rambler
(2.30) and Outpoint (3.0) ap-

Ver

Their verdict,
of the leading b
sentatives on the

Ladbroke
ted £250,00
versy amon
n was show
erly disapp
d that h
ht the
In contras
es I woul

his blushe
of that da
showed t
ure a run fo
was plainly su
resources, th y
"flatten" Grevil
Lightning Record
lucky to

COMING TO THE LAST

A Tribute to Peter O'Sullevan

COMING TO THE LAST

A TRIBUTE TO
PETER O'SULLEVAN

EDITED BY
Sean Magee

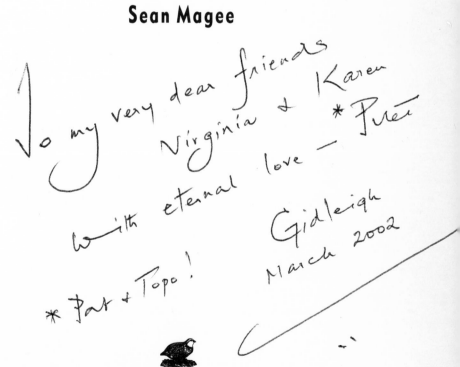

To my very dear friends Virginia & Karen with eternal love — Peter *Pat + Topo! Gidleigh March 2002

PARTRIDGE PRESS

LONDON · NEW YORK · TORONTO · SYDNEY · AUCKLAND

TRANSWORLD PUBLISHERS LTD
61-63 Uxbridge Road, London W5 5SA

TRANSWORLD PUBLISHERS (AUSTRALIA) PTY LTD
15-25 Helles Avenue, Moorebank, NSW 2170

TRANSWORLD PUBLISHERS (NZ) LTD
3 William Pickering Drive, Albany, Auckland

Published 1997 by Partridge Press
a division of Transworld Publishers Ltd

ISBN 185225 2634

Typeset by Production Line, Minster Lovell, Oxford.
Printed in Great Britain by Mackays of Chatham PLC, Chatham, Kent.

Contents

Foreword

Anyone who has attempted to interpret the horse racing scene for more than half a century, as I have been privileged to do, should be inured to total dismay. I thought I was – until now. When the publishers of this volume commissioned a similar work in respect of the more renowned commentator Brian Johnston, 'Johnners' (as he was affectionately known) took the precaution of moderating potential embarrassment by predeceasing publication.

Under different circumstances, what can I do but express my eternal thanks to Sean Magee for his shameless, assiduous pursuit of comment on my modest career; to Transworld Publishers and their enthusiastic team who inspired the research; and, of course, to the gracious and benevolent contributors whose response reflects the degree to which the hoofbeat of the racehorse resonates in the heart of his admirers?

PETER O'SULLEVAN

Preface

Like so many of the contributors to this book, I grew up to the sound of Peter O'Sullevan's voice, and like so many I felt from the start that I had a personal involvement with him. I held him directly responsible for letting Arkle scoot away from Mill House in the 1964 Cheltenham Gold Cup, but since those days I have learned not to berate the messenger who brings bad news – even when he brought the worst news of all, Crisp being caught by Red Rum in 1973 – and instead to appreciate the immense influence which Peter has had on racing for the last half century.

His initial diffidence when approached about this project was worn down by the prospect of royalties being channelled towards his favourite charities, and his cooperation – dispensed with a sort of bemused benevolence – has been invaluable as the book was put together, as has his willingness to let me rampage through his cutting books and fan mail. My grateful thanks to him, and to all the contributors who have been so ready and willing to pay him tribute.

SEAN MAGEE

SANDRINGHAM, NORFOLK

I am pleased to have this opportunity to record my appreciation of
Peter O'Sullevan's distinguished contribution to racing during these last fifty years.
I recall particularly his help and advice to me in making the television film "The
Queen's Racehorses" in the 1970s. But his very special accomplishment has been in
his role as presenter and above all commentator, instantly recognisable and always
bringing the thrill and excitement of the racecourse to us through radio and television;
his is one of the great voices of British racing. I send my good wishes to him for a
long and happy retirement.

ELIZABETH R.

January, 1997.

My earliest recollection of Peter O'Sullevan was of the voice
which was not to be interrupted on a Saturday afternoon.

My home town is Ballina in the West of Ireland where, in the
Sixties, television reception from the UK was almost non-
existent. Nevertheless, it provided a lifeline for a family
passionately interested in racing. On televised racing days,
meals were rushed and there was a dash by my father and four
brothers for their seats in front of the television.

Nearby stood an ancient wireless, the domain of Michael
O'Hehir, the doyen of Irish sports broadcasting. When the
television was turned on, invariably to a hissing, snowy
scene, there would be frantic efforts to tune into the sound
as the moment of the 'off' approached. A hand apparently more
suited to grasping a rugby ball than a small dial would
expertly manipulate the signal: a faint crackle assumed a
pattern and then, miraculously, there would be a voice, very
faint but unmistakable. "That's it!", "That's Peter
O'Sullevan!", "Come on, O'Sullevan!". A few more delicate,
almost imperceptible turns and then ". . . coming up on the
outside, turning his head to accept the adulation of the
crowd, is Arkle! And Mill House is desperately trying to stay
in touch . . .".

Five large men sat enthralled, watching the racing, seeing
every horse, the brilliance of the jockeys' silks, the mighty
leaps, the cracking falls, the bookies and the crowds - thanks
to the genius of Peter O'Sullevan and that wonderful voice,
because, on the screen, there was nothing but a blinding
blizzard of static! And more than once I heard the comment
"that man really knows his horses"!

On behalf of many Irish men and women, I say go raibh mile
maith agat, and every good wish to Peter for a long and happy
retirement.

MARY ROBINSON
Uachtaran na hEireann

CLARENCE HOUSE
S.W.1

Over the past fifty years
Peter O'Sullevan has thrilled and
excited me and countless other
racegoers with his commentaries.
His knowledge, memory, clarity of
speech and sense of the occasion
have enabled him to reach the
pinnacle of his profession, and
I send him my warmest good wishes
for the future.

ELIZABETH R
Queen Mother

January 1997

BROADCAST

FROM THE CHIEF EXECUTIVE, BBC BROADCAST

BRITISH BROADCASTING CORPORATION
BROADCASTING HOUSE
PORTLAND PLACE
LONDON W1A 1AA
TELEPHONE: 0171-580 4468

There are very few broadcasters who over time become synonymous with the sport they cover. Peter O'Sullevan is such a one. Indeed, his name heads any roll call of such broadcasters.

He is the most courteous and dignified of men; the most accurate and skilful of commentators. I remember, as a young man, marvelling as he went twice through the <u>entire</u> Derby field of nearly thirty runners before they had reached Tattenham Corner. He remains the best caller of a finish, as even his competitors will agree.

One of his greatest achievements was to conduct an impeccable commentary on the Grand National that never was, calling the horses while simultaneously telling viewers that this was a contest which would not count - broadcasting skills, journalism, experience and authority combined in one racing man as in no other.

When the tapes go up at Aintree on April 5th, as we sincerely hope they do, Peter will achieve a milestone which will not be passed again - his fiftieth Grand National commentary.

On behalf of the BBC, and more importantly, on behalf of the millions of BBC viewers who have enjoyed and benefited from his work, I offer my thanks to a great sportsman and a great broadcaster.

Will Wyatt

1

'The bugger's just never wrong'

Peter O'Sullevan the man

" She monopolises racing and snocker on BBC and the soap operas on ITV but never puts a penny in the kitty for the licence"

The bare facts: Peter O'Sullevan was born in County Kerry on 3 March 1918; joined the Press Association as racing correspondent in 1944, wrote for the Daily Express *from 1950 to 1986, and for* Today *1986–7; began race broadcasting for the BBC in 1946, and commentated on the first televised Grand National in 1960; has owned several racehorses, notably Be Friendly and Attivo; was elected to the Jockey Club in 1986; was awarded the OBE in 1976, and the CBE in 1991; has won numerous awards as journalist, owner and commentator, and for his work on behalf of various charities; published his best-selling autobiography* Calling the Horses *in 1989; announced in November 1996 that he would be retiring from commentary in November 1997.*

Now for the man behind those facts . . .

Of all the articles written about Peter O'Sullevan over the decades, the most famous – and most quoted – is the piece by Hugh McIlvanney, doyen of British sports journalists, first published in The Observer in December 1973 under the title 'Calling the horses home'.

Hugh McIlvanney

Peter O'Sullevan is widely accepted as the best horse-racing commentator in the history of broadcasting, and possibly the most accomplished reader of action operating on any sport in the English-speaking world. His admirers are convinced that had he been on the rails at Balaclava he would have kept pace with the Charge of the Light Brigade, listing the fallers in precise order and describing the riders' injuries before they hit the ground.

'Compared with him,' said Lester Piggott, 'all the rest are amateurs.' Obviously it would be naïve to expect a contrary opinion from Brian Cowgill, Head of BBC Sport and Outside Broadcasts, who has fought long and successfully to guard his star against the wooing attentions of independent television. But Cowgill's enthusiasm is of a kind that cannot be explained by self-interest. He sounds as close to being awed as a Lancastrian could be when he says: 'I've worked with O'Sullevan, man and boy, for twenty-five years and I've never known the bugger to be wrong. The man is an experts' expert. There are many others who have more to say before and after a race, but while the horses are running he is on his own, without a rival. Between the starting stalls and the winning line Peter is Holy Writ. I tell you, the bugger's just never wrong.'

On hearing such a tribute at second hand, O'Sullevan winces behind the heavy rims of his glasses. 'It's marvellous that one's guv'nor should say things like that, and I won't be sending any letters of protest to Brian, but of course it's all bull really. My own awareness of just how fallible I am makes me try like hell to take out insurance against disaster. I go to all sorts of lengths to get a proof of the racecard the night before a meeting, then I paste it on to cardboard and draw in the silks of the owners in coloured pencil opposite each horse. In some races over the jumps, where the fields are large and many of the animals and their riders comparatively unknown, the process of memorizing can be desperate. Maybe I overdo the homework but I don't want to leave myself any excuse for a balls-up. I'm terrible for forgetting people's names at parties but I always say that if they came in wearing crossbelts and a spotted cap I'd get them right without any trouble.'

Neither his own thoroughness nor the absolute faith of those who work with him can relieve O'Sullevan of the nervous agony that has always accompanied his preparation for major commentaries. He no longer has the severe attacks of diarrhoea he once endured, often right up to starting time, but says he is not beyond having a mild case of the trots, especially before a Grand National. 'That one always gets me choked up, far more so than a Derby or anything else on the Flat. Mind you, it would be impossible for me not to get excited watching any horse race. I think it is so beautiful, so dramatic. That's one reason I'm glad to have a special viewing apparatus with a powerful pair of naval binoculars fixed into metal supports and angled lenses that allow me to stand and look down into them. I always read a race direct through glasses, not from a screen, but if I tried to hold a pair of bins they would vibrate in my hands as if electricity was going through them.'

Fortunately for everyone interested in racing, he keeps coming up for the next ordeal, and not merely because of the £175 a day the BBC pay him on a minimum of forty working days a year. As a prodigiously informed and experienced racing journalist (his partnership with Clive Graham in the *Daily Express* is reckoned by our own award-winner Richard Baerlein to represent the highest standard of work in the field) he shares the frustrations of many another newspaperman and says that broadcasting offers an excellent release. The technicians who find themselves targets for O'Sullevan's impatience are rewarded by his almost flawless performances, consoled by the certainty that he is harder on himself than on anyone else. He goes on his twice-yearly holidays in the knowledge that his last few nights away from commentating will be marred by recurring nightmares about his return. 'In my dreams a race is suddenly being led by a horse that should not be there, one I have never seen before. Or it may be worse and I will see twenty totally unfamiliar horses, twenty anonymous sets of riding silks coming towards me. I wake up in a sweat.' These glimpses of black apprehension will astonish many among the millions of racing enthusiasts who regard him as Mr Cool, a man whose voice can stay calm, mellifluous and charged with relevant information in the most hectic finish – and did so even when his own great sprinter Be Friendly was getting up to win £5,000 by a short head. But Peter O'Sullevan has been in deeper tunnels, darker places, than those provided by dreams.

Seeing him now at fifty-five, a tall, slim, handsome figure, with his silver hair swept back from a strong profile and down on to the velvet collar of his overcoat, a man who catches the eye of most women and instantly commands the deferential attentions of waiters, it is hard to believe there were years when he sought the shadows as resolutely as the Phantom of the Opera. Those years, when his face and his confidence were blighted by a virulent form of acne, shaped his view of life. They created the paradox of an apparently remote personality, a natural loner who drives from the racecourse in his Jaguar almost before the sweat has dried on the horses and yet is vibrant company for anyone who penetrates the outer stockade. Strangely, considering that it was ability on the football field that swung his admission into Charterhouse, he suffered from asthma even before leaving his birthplace in County Kerry. At the age of sixteen he was taken to Switzerland, where he acquired the French that has been so useful to him ever since and found some ease from asthma. Sadly, the nervous implications of that disease culminated in the outbreak of acne. It became so bad that he spent most of one year in the Middlesex Hospital.

'They wanted me to leave because they couldn't do any more for me, but I didn't want to go. Once out of the hospital, I used to find the coffee bars and milk bars where the lights were dimmest. I could still take on most taxi drivers when it comes to knowledge of London. That was an indescribably painful period of my life but I am convinced that a serious illness, for anyone who comes out of it in reasonable shape, can be a profoundly enriching experience. It forces you back on your own resources, makes you examine yourself and your life more honestly than you might otherwise do. My experiences, for instance, took me further into literature than I might ever have been and taught me an appreciation of the visual arts which may not be acute but is an important sustaining element in my life. Having no direct communication with fellow human beings, I resorted to inanimate forms of communication such as painting. I still find visiting galleries a marvellous restorative, far better than going for a drink. And I say that as someone who loves wine.'

The love of wine and the love of art are equally in evidence in the flat in Chelsea where O'Sullevan lives with his wife Pat and their poodle. Some of his favourite pictures he bought from his friend John Skeaping after they got skint at White City dogs thirty-two years ago. He met Pat rather later, in 1946, long after what happened to him as an ambulance driver with the Rescue Service during the Blitz had begun his progress towards a cure. 'I was rated as a daredevil but the truth is that at first I didn't care whether or not a bomb or building fell on me. Then I realized that other people could be nervous, that I could have the respect of other people, and I began to come out and lead a full life.'

He has certainly done that in the last twenty years. His career as a racing journalist, which he had already decided upon by the age of eight, and as a broadcaster, which he jeopardized by tossing a bemused BBC executive double or nothing over the terms of his first contract, have both flourished. As a racehorse owner (an interest that developed naturally when he realized he wasn't the greatest rider in the world) he graduated from a succession of hilarious mishaps to a partnership in Be Friendly. That flyer won eleven races, dead-heated for another, collected £44,000 in prizes, brought O'Sullevan half as much when he sold a quarter share and has given the compulsive punter in him quite a few bonuses. Be Friendly is now a high-earning stallion. 'My luck with him,' says the part-owner, 'has been miraculous.'

O'Sullevan, however, will be remembered as someone who describes other people's triumphs, as the man whose voice is the most precise focusing mechanism in sport, the perfect instrument for putting names and personalities to the blurred rainbow of a big racing field. But there is a strong spirit behind the voice, as some drunken critics of Lester Piggott discovered at Longchamp when they accosted O'Sullevan after Nijinsky's defeat in the Arc. 'Well, Peter, did Lester make a boo-boo?' they asked. He had just seen a great friend and a great racehorse beaten and his customary affability deserted him. So did his microphone voice. "**** off," I said. And I felt better for it.'

Most of us feel better for hearing Peter O'Sullevan, but maybe those fellows were an exception.

Brough Scott, now a leading racing journalist but previously an amateur and then professional jockey, recalls an early encounter with 'the wolf that walked alone'.

Brough Scott

He used to hang away from the pack. A quiet, attentive figure in trilby and short grey-brown overcoat, the eyes inscrutable behind the tinted glasses. Everyone knew the voice, the most famous sound in British racing, but this was Peter O'Sullevan the journalist, the wolf that walked alone.

He was the man who had made contacts into an art form. He knew everyone from barons to barrow boys, from spivs to superstars. He would be just as much at ease discussing French Classic form (in French) with Yves Saint-Martin as poring over the merits of a seller at Southwell. No guesses in which guise I first met him.

By any normal journalistic standards the nine-race card at Southwell that Monday, 16 December 1963, was about as insignificant as you could get, and the nineteen-runner Burgage Selling Handicap Hurdle could therefore be deemed the lowliest of the low. Even now, the idea that it or anything on that drizzly winter's day should attract the attention of the great man who forty-eight hours earlier had been calling Scottish Memories home at Cheltenham seems beyond belief. But the wolf was on the prowl.

He would hunt round the little meetings just as diligently as he would the big. There would be confidences to be gained, stories to be found, even bets to be played. Come to think of it, Peter was probably playing that day at Southwell. He certainly seemed to know an awful lot about the form and the trainer of Blue Peak, an old crock of former talent who had just made me feel like Lester Piggott himself. It had never been like this before. It was a day of which you recall every purring minute.

True, they are all blurred together. What seemed like the endless drive northwards, a student in a mini-van rendered somewhat unwelcoming by its use for transporting the canisters of wolf urine we used as 'scent' for the Oxford Draghounds; the enormity of changing and going out to ride against what seemed so battle-hardened a bunch of professionals; the 'beginner's luck' confidence which meant that until proved different I would believe Blue Peak was Pegasus revisited – and in the race he felt just that; the ecstatic triumph being led back to the winner's circle; the little cameo while the trainer clucked his teeth and theatrically unpeeled Blue Peak's bandages to put off would-be bidders; the sit-down in the sanctuary of the weighing room; and then the summons from O'Sullevan.

He must have done this thousands and thousands of times. But the trick was the interest. The granting of importance (however ill-deserved) to the interviewee. The seeming privacy of the quiet conversation in an openly public place. The sense that you were understood. It was a trick he did all on his own. Over the years one saw more of it, but the essential hunger lessened not a jot. *Daily Express* readers would know that if other papers had racing stories in front of them, they would be very, very few. The amount of work, the amount of mileage, must have been phenomenal. But it was less than half of the O'Sullevan story. To my great good fortune, I was also to have first-hand experience of the other side.

It was the summer of 1970. The riding had gone far better than I could have dared to hope, but not as well as dreams would have it. The right ankle had been rearranged at Worcester and there were long dead months on crutches. Then a light beckoned in the commentary box. It meant, one afternoon at Newbury in August, that I was to work alongside Peter O'Sullevan. This was a different game, and he a different player. There was the same generosity of spirit, in his kind introductions and his supportive comments to what was a truly terrified first-time performer. But there was also a necessary outward élan which was hidden in the almost shy manner he went about getting his scoops and stories. He may have always been a bit reserved in front of camera but the voice had to take control, and close up there was an almost tangible reassurance in hearing it on the headphones. It's a voice that has to lead and to share. It has a style and a cut to it which demand attention in the most well-bred way. It is a Savile Row voice, and the only problem with working alongside it that well-remembered day was being aware of the shoddiness of one's own enunciation in comparison. Twenty-seven years on, the comparison still fails to flatter.

Our broadcasting paths parted when ITV kindly offered to subsidize the Scott expenses, but we shared commentary boxes in various unlikely spots, none more unnerving than that right atop the main stand at The Curragh on the day a bomb scare evacuated every racegoer on the track. It was one thing to describe the incongruity of a 30,000 crowd assembled for inspection way below us, quite another to realize that we and our engineers were the only humans unwise enough not to join them. Could it be that the others knew something we didn't? Needless to say, the seamless BBC description betrayed no sense of imminent demolition. Wish I could say the same about their rival's.

So down the years the O'Sullevan public voice has continued to inspire, to be the benchmark whereby all other racing commentaries are judged. But a final memory is again of the more private journalistic side, and is remarkable in that he bothered to call at all. The place was a discreet nursing home otherwise used as an abortion clinic. I had been taken there not for that reason but on clearance from Warwick Hospital after a back injury which had ended my not particularly distinguished race-riding career. Discreet screens were no barrier to O'Sullevan. His voice came over the line, quietly picking over the bits of what in the scheme of things was an extremely unimportant story. But there was something wonderfully encouraging in his interest. For me as for many others, he had been the first and the last. He was Alpha and Omega. He was the leader of the pack.

A measure of Peter O'Sullevan's stature is how he is appreciated by professionals from other fields. Robin Oakley, the BBC's political editor, is an enthusiastic racing fan who has channelled that enthusiasm into a weekly column on the Turf in The Spectator.

Robin Oakley

A seven-pound claimer among racing writers, I found myself at the 1996 Lesters at the same table as the two men who had done most over the years, without my ever meeting them until then, to foster my love of racing. Becalmed on that desert island without a betting shack or even a crab-racing track, I would be torn for my one permitted book between *Oaksey on Racing* and Peter O'Sullevan's *Calling the Horses*. And there they were, heads together like two wise old birds on a branch, largely oblivious for much of the time of their fellow diners. Typically, I learned from Peter later, he and John Oaksey had been discussing their latest racing charity project. And it is that readiness to give back to the sport, and to those characters, human and equine, who risk life and limb in providing it, which distinguishes them both.

If Peter O'Sullevan has contributed lavishly to my racing education, his contribution to my normal learning was less approved by the powers that be. More than once in my schooldays I suffered for my teachers' discovery of the *Express* racing page, discreetly folded, among the set texts of the day as I devoured the latest example of O'Sullevan prose, a reminder even then of Matthew Arnold's comment that the best journalism is simply 'literature in a hurry'. A fellow enthusiast and I were so carried away with his efforts on one occasion, and with the serious business of Royal Ascot selections, that there was little time left for the essay project. The headmaster's comment on what resulted was pithy: 'Well, Oakley. So long as they have a point I do not mind long essays or short ones. What I do object to is receiving what is no more than a random selection from the *Oxford Dictionary of Quotations*, cobbled together with the aid of the few conjunctions you happen to know.' Thank you, Peter.

No man has done more than Peter O'Sullevan to make racing live for those of us who cannot be at the trackside as often as we would like. Most of racing's great moments in my lifetime are associated with word pictures he has drawn, with drama unfolded at speed in that marvellous honeyed gravel voice, the emphases timed with the instinctive artistry of a Scobie Breasley challenge. Perhaps those who know him better could spot in an inflexion here or a pause there some hint of which fading favourite or final-furlong challenger was carrying the additional penalty of the O'Sullevan ante-post voucher. But it has never been apparent to me in the commentaries of a man who, had he chosen the political sphere instead, would never have earned the accusation of partiality.

His contacts are clearly unrivalled. His professionalism is without question. Just note how often in his memoirs he is taking time out in some exotic spot to spend the necessary hours mugging up the colours for the next day's race-calling. And always there is that deftness with the anecdote, as when George Moore sought to get some experience of Epsom before riding an Alec Head Derby favourite and was offered the ride on O'Sullevan's Chinchilla in a seller. The saddle slipped and Moore was deposited heavily on to the Epsom turf 200 yards short of the line, where he lay prone. By the time the worried owner reached him he was sitting up, saying: 'Sorry, I hadn't meant to feel the course with my head.' The riderless O'Sullevan horse meanwhile careered into a saddling box where Head's favourite for the next race was being prepared. 'Not content with nearly killing my jockey,' said the trainer, 'you try to finish off my horse as well.' The best journalists have that capacity to have things happen *to* them as well.

But what strikes one most is Peter O'Sullevan's instinctive feeling for horse and rider, his natural 'sens du cheval'. It is that which has made him such an effective campaigner. Think back over the years. In the 1960s he was one of the leading voices calling for the introduction of starting stalls in Britain after they had been first tried in France. 'Over my dead body,' said a lot of his stuffier trainer friends. But he persevered and in due course the authorities paid some attention to the start as well as the finish of races. In the late 1970s, Peter O'Sullevan's was one of the earliest and strongest voices demanding action to rid courses of the spectacle of demented jockeys pointlessly thrashing beaten horses, seeking restrictions on both the size and the use of the whip. The success of the campaign so far has done much to educate riders, trainers and the watching public, to the benefit of those magnificent animals who give us all such pleasure. And for many years, well before it became a fashionable cause for television documentary-makers, Peter O'Sullevan has played a wider role in the welfare both of horses whose racing days are done and of others who have never enjoyed what is generally the five-star hotel pampering that is the lot of the racing Thoroughbred.

It tells us one thing about Peter's lifestyle that the one campaign he refused to join was Lord Beaverbrook's sudden enthusiasm in the 1960s for the abolition of bookmaking. He has preferred the more traditional way of trying to get back at the old enemy. It tells us rather more about him that the last sentence in my well-thumbed copy of *Calling the Horses* concludes with a reference to 'those whose aim is to add the missing letter "e" to the human race'. That he certainly helps to do.

Dick Francis's most notorious moment in the saddle – the collapse of the Queen Mother's Devon Loch fifty yards from certain victory in the 1956 Grand National – occurred four years before BBC Television had started covering the race. But the Francis and O'Sullevan paths had crossed long before then, when Peter was broadcasting on the 1949 Grand National which saw Dick Francis's first ride in the race.

Dick Francis

Fame depends on the chroniclers. Dr Johnson, the dictionary-writing genius, would be merely a footnote without Boswell. Any intrepid explorer could have discovered the source of the Nile fifty times without anyone caring were it not for the journalist Stanley's immortal politeness in the vastness of the jungle: 'Dr Livingstone, I presume?'

One can't say horse racing wouldn't exist without its chroniclers, but its historic triumphs, its heroes, its myths and its lasting legends are all the gifts of the enthusiastic and perceptive few who saw, understood and wrote it down. Peter O'Sullevan began to give vivid life to the steeple-chasing scene at the time when I myself was actively engaged in soaring over as much black birch as possible. National Hunt racing was not at that time a widely recognized sport. The public knew a bit about the Grand National (chiefly because of the Irish Sweepstake lottery on the result) but often thought it occurred in a vacuum as the only jumping race of the year. Peter O'Sullevan and television changed all that.

When I rode in my first Grand National in 1949 Peter O'Sullevan, in his early thirties, was making one of his earliest broadcasts on that race. In century terms, as a chronicler he followed Meyrick Good and was a contemporary for a long time with Tom Nickalls, Julian Simcocks and Bill Curling. He became one whose facts one could trust, whose judgement was fair and informed, whose comments didn't prompt howls of rage with furiously crumpled newspapers being hurled across trainers' breakfast tables. Jockeys found that pilot error was seldom blamed in the O'Sullevan columns. Here was a commentator who understood split-second decisions at speed with one's life on the line. He never coldly dissected with unfriendly hindsight the unwise move or the failure to find an opening which might have won a race. Peter, instead, praised the winner.

More than that, if he ever inadvertently learned something that might have made a good story but would harm or embarrass the people involved, he would hold it back, unpublished. I rode for a trainer – Peter Cazalet – who hated the press to know anything about his affairs. Peter O'Sullevan asked me one day if something he'd learned by accident about one of the Cazalet horses was true. It was, but I begged him in some desperation not to print it (as it would have caused endless ill-will) and he didn't. I don't suppose he remembers, but I do, and I still think it remarkable.

It is odd, now that the chroniclers and the chronicled are seen with their arms round each others' shoulders, to recall that back in the fifties the professionals engaged in racing considered the press to be the enemy from whom all information should be withheld. When in 1957 I accepted the offer of a column in the *Sunday Express* I felt I was becoming a traitor to my past. Some trainers I'd ridden for were, indeed, horrified, but to his great credit Peter Cazalet, the most private of them all, opened his stable yard to my pen and gave me trust; and I tried, like Peter O'Sullevan, never to step where I would do harm.

Peter O'Sullevan rode to national recognition with the growth of television. His voice became as familiar as Big Ben, and with his *Daily Express* colleague, Clive Graham, he formed a writing and broadcasting partnership that was as lighthearted and entertaining as any double act, and was reliable besides. When Clive died of cancer in 1974 a light went out in racing. Peter has never found another such partner; perhaps there isn't one.

Apart from illuminating the whole sport from Epsom to Ascot to Aintree, Peter also owns horses himself. I rode for him once when Fred Winter was injured: the horse was called The Solid Man, it hit the solid birch and I ended on the solid ground – but this debacle seemed not to extinguish the real friendship that has quietly lasted between us through all our parallel lives.

I once listened in fascination to Peter race-reading the Daily Express Triumph Hurdle at the Cheltenham Festival. His own great four-year-old, Attivo, won the race magnificently and Peter's voice relayed the result as calmly as usual: 'Attivo the winner . . . owned by Peter O'Sullevan . . .'

Peter, the winner. That says it all.

Mike Dillon, Director of Public Relations for Ladbrokes, recalls two contrasting Grand National memories, separated by twenty-seven years.

Mike Dillon

Hare and Hounds Hotel, Middleton, Manchester; 3.17 p.m., 26 March 1966:

As a fourteen-year-old who was already taking sport too seriously, I knew that something special was happening. My father's public house was next door to a bookmaker's shop, so Saturday was always a busy day. But this was different. The fists were bouncing on the table with greater resonance. The shouting and cheering were louder, but a distinctive voice was cutting through the clouds of smoke, creating the atmosphere, making the adrenaline pump. The shilling each way that I had been allowed to place on Anglo at 50–1 meant that racing, and in particular the Grand National, had a new devotee. It would be much later that I would fully understand what was meant by 'The Voice of Racing' and have the privilege of meeting the man who was responsible for making the hearts in my home town of Middleton beat faster.

Ladbrokes gave me the opportunity to become fully involved in the Grand National when they rescued it from what now seems unthinkable obscurity in 1976. Arriving at a silent, cold Aintree in December 1975 and having to locate a key to the derelict grandstand, I wondered if the cheers would ever again call a winner past the Elbow. Fortunately I was inspired by meeting the great man. He infected me with his enthusiasm and would subsequently tell me that his favourite Nationals were Red Rum's third victory in 1977 and Aldaniti's emotional triumph in 1981. Peter O'Sullevan says that his greatest fear is calling the wrong horse home and being remembered for it. He will be remembered, in fact, for far different reasons, and it was my respect for his amazing knowledge and expertise that guided me through one of the most difficult and potentially disastrous moments of my career in the world of bookmaking.

*

Press Room, Aintree, 3.50 p.m., 3 April 1993:

'The red flag has been raised . . . '

 'False start . . .'

 'The tape is around Dunwoody's neck . . .'

 'This is one of the greatest sensations in Grand National history . . . nine horses are left at the start . . .'

These were the words which were again cutting through the noisier than usual press room at Aintree. This, as with everything involving the National, was different. As the posse of journalists were trying to digest what was unfolding I was tapped on the shoulder by Owen Thomas, the BBC outside broadcast stage manager, who simply beckoned me to follow him. He pushed his way impatiently through the crowd, looking round only to inform me that Des Lynam needed to know what was happening to all bets.

Now it was my turn to experience the adrenaline and Peter O'Sullevan's words were going through my head like machine-gun fire: 'They are going to have to pull up . . . It is impossible for any other outcome . . . This is the National that certainly isn't.'

A total of £75 million was sitting in betting offices all over the country and the only question the punters wanted answered was: would it be returned to them? Des Lynam was giving a performance which would later help him win a BAFTA award for remaining cool under pressure. Although I had been interviewed on television many times before, this had to be my biggest audience. I answered the question: the race was void, all money to be returned. Peter O'Sullevan had helped and guided me again. He had proved once more that he understood racing so thoroughly, so naturally, that he could be relied upon to bring clarity to its most confusing moments.

As a bookmaking man, I own up to the hope that Peter will call another 50–1 winner for me on his last National. More personally, I know for sure that without his magnificent commentary the race cannot possibly be the same again.

John Oaksey, one of the 'two wise old birds on a branch' described by Robin Oakley in his piece earlier in this section and one of the most influential and informed racing writers of the age, wrote of 'Racing's debt to O'Sullevan' in the Racing Post shortly after the publication of Peter O'Sullevan's autobiography Calling the Horses in 1989.

John Oaksey

The last chapter of Peter O'Sullevan's enthralling autobiography *Calling the Horses* suggests that the debt of gratitude he owes to horses is 'still accumulating'. Maybe it is. But no one remotely interested in what Phil Bull used to call 'the great triviality' can read this lovely book without recognizing that, when you talk of gratitude it is we, the racing world, who are, overwhelmingly, in debt.

There are at least two huge slices of good fortune for which we should be thankful. The first and by far the largest is that, for the best part of sixty years, this extraordinary, many-sided man has chosen to work and write and commentate his heart out for our entertainment. And the other, I'm delighted to say, is that, thanks, mainly, to Peter's own patience, judgement and talent for friendship, his sincere and lifelong love of horses has, in the end, been both returned and, at least in terms of pleasure and excitement, handsomely repaid.

Be Friendly and Attivo may only have come after twenty years of unprofitable and mostly unsuccessful selling-plater ownership. But no one can read the vivid accounts of their careers – or recall the super-human *sangfroid* with which their triumphs were described on air – without knowing that, as Peter would certainly agree, fate did, occasionally, give him the sort of reward he richly deserved.

Jack Leach began *Sods I Have Cut On The Turf* (beside which, along with George Lambton's *Men and Horses I Have Known*, Peter's book deserves a place on any racing bookshelf) by denying that he was ever a 'horse lover'. The only horse Jack ever loved, he claimed, was a pony who, if you threw the reins over her head, stood quite still while you got off to pick mushrooms. Fairy, on whom Peter O'Sullevan galloped round Tattenham Corner in 1925, sounds a bit lively for mushroom-picking – but never mind. His owner–rider was, and has been ever since, a horse lover in the best and completest sense of that often misused term. Almost the only bitter or angry passages in Peter's book concern cruelty to horses. Most of us vaguely *feel* that way, of course – but he has got up and done something about it. With the help of the International League for the Protection of Horses, he personally inspired the setting up of a clinic for maltreated ponies in Morocco and, in a whole series of campaigns against abuse of the whip, doping and unfair obstacles, against the export for meat of unwanted horses and in favour of their humane destruction in familiar surroundings, Peter's pen, voice, charm and influence have been resolutely employed.

It was he, I remember, who first pointed out to me the unfairness of the slope on the landing side of Becher's Brook. I had been whingeing away for ages about how the old water jump could unfairly catch and injure horses, without realizing that the Becher's 'lip' was just as unfair a trap. Well, now both are gone and for those, as for so many other humane improvements, Peter deserves the lion's share of credit.

The chief blessing, of course, for his readers, viewers and listeners – indeed, for the racing world as a whole – is that, almost ever since the war, Peter has been actively, often hectically, involved, closer to the professional summit and centre of that world than any other single human being I can think of. To say that he has a 'talent for friendship' is a serious understatement. I cannot think of anyone who has been liked, respected and trusted by a wider variety of racing professionals, and numerous amateurs as well. Who placed bets for Vincent O'Brien, Aly Khan and, often unwisely, for that eternal optimist Paddy Prendergast? Who shared the confidence (well, sometimes, anyway) of remote Gallic geniuses like François Mathet and Etienne Pollet? Who refused an offer of £5 from the young Lester Piggott and proposed Michael Stoute as BBC racing correspondent? The list goes on and on, and, looking down it, you can easily understand how regularly those 'scoops' used to appear in 'Off the Record' and Peter's other *Express* columns.

But essential required reading though those pieces were – and apart, of course, from his matchless commentaries – I suspect that it is as a tipster and provider of advanced ante-post information that Peter O'Sullevan best served his huge public, and as which, perhaps, he would also like to be remembered. He has always been a bold, assiduous, and, on balance, I suspect, a pretty successful punter. 'I notice he never says how much *he* used to win!' Lester Piggott said with a broad grin when Peter's book was launched – at the Ritz, where else? – the other night. Their friendship goes back to a day when Keith Piggott asked Peter to give the thirteen-year-old future champion a lift to the races. A lot of punters have gone broke following the advice of jockeys but the friendship of Lester, Rae Johnstone, Scobie Breasley and many other great jockeys meant that Peter's tips were often based on genuine 'information'.

The only item of that kind I was ever, personally, able to pass on was when a horse called The Bugler ran so well first time out at Cheltenham that Terry Biddlecombe, finishing beside us on Comedy Of Errors, asked 'to be told when that one's off!' While absolutely denying the regrettable implication of the champion jockey's words, I repeated them to Peter as a supposedly funny story. Three weeks later, with The Bugler due to run at Sandown, imagine my surprise to be got out of bed at my club on the morning of the race to take a call from Mr O'Sullevan. 'Does he mind the soft ground?', the great man wanted to know, and quite rightly, took no notice of my rather discouraging reply. Because in we went at 33–1, backed, presumably, by Bert at the garage and all the other lucky *Express* readers. How brilliantly they were served.

Besides cruelty and odds-cutting bookmakers, another thing Peter always hated was unfairness. Happily for him the Jockey Club, of which he is now a member, does not contain many autocrats like the late Lord Rosebery, to whom justice seems to have mattered a good deal less than his own office and opinions. (I speak from bitter personal experience because the noble Earl tried to get me the sack for writing that a filly he had in the Sales was ungenuine!) Peter tells, with disgust, the sad story of Charles Chapman, one, and by no means the last, of the trainer-martyrs ruined by the old doping rules. It is good to know that, if any such hateful processes should now even be suggested in the corridors of power, the familiar, well-loved voice which has thrilled us on so many great racing occasions for half a century will speak out loud and clear against them.

Like John Oaksey, Vincent O'Brien, who retired in 1994 after arguably the finest training career of modern times, has enjoyed an association with Peter O'Sullevan which goes back many decades.

Vincent O'Brien

I have admired Peter from the first time I heard him commentating on a race, nearly fifty years ago, and I am very proud to be able to count him among my best friends. We have seen each other not only on the racecourse but during skiing holidays – Peter was a very fine skier – as well as meeting regularly on my trips to England, when Peter and Pat have been marvellous hosts of the most superb dinner parties at their flat in Chelsea.

On a professional level, Peter has contributed so much to the prestige of racing. Some pressmen can be too forthright in their criticism, especially when they are not aware of all the facts in a situation, but I have never heard Peter say an unkind word about anyone. He has always been unvaryingly dignified and the excellence of English racing itself has been greatly enhanced by him. His outstanding commentaries set the mood for so many of the big racing occasions such as Royal Ascot, Cheltenham and the Grand National. The pitch, tone and resonance of his voice are quite unique and recognizable worldwide.

Peter's profound knowledge of the sport had more tangible benefits, too: he was such a shrewd punter that he could always get the best available odds about a horse and then perhaps the occasional point better!

When Ballymoss was running in the Prix de l'Arc de Triomphe at Longchamp in 1958 I asked Peter to place a large ante-post bet for me. We knew Ballymoss to be a colt of the highest class – he had won the Irish Derby and English St Leger in 1957 and the Eclipse, Coronation Cup and King George VI and Queen Elizabeth Stakes earlier in the 1958 season. My one worry about the horse was that he needed good to firm ground and was not at his most effective on the soft. I had good reason for this feeling: Ballymoss's last run as a two-year-old was on soft ground at The Curragh and he disappointed. His first run at three, again at The Curragh, was on heavy ground and he finished down the field. In his prep race for the St Leger, the Great Voltigeur Stakes at York, the ground was soft and again he ran way below his form. Admittedly the going had been a little soft when he won the St Leger itself, but I was still unhappy about him showing his best under testing conditions at Longchamp. When on Arc day, a few hours before the off, it started to pour down, I became very depressed.

Peter was commentating on the Arc for the BBC, so I tracked him down: Ballymoss's chance was receding with every further minute of the downpour. Was there any chance of laying off the bet? He said he'd see what he could do . . .

When Scobie Breasley, who was due to ride Ballymoss, came in after riding in the second race and shook his head at me as he passed, my gloom deepened; then my spirits sank even further when I encountered Peter again just before the big race. He had been unable to lay off the bet: it would have to stand. Oh well, that's that, I thought – but then Ballymoss and Scobie, following a 'line' proposed by his and Peter's great friend Rae Johnstone, sluiced through the mud to win by two lengths. The pre-race doubts were forgotten in the excitement of my first Arc win. Victory in the Arc was much more important than any bet; but the great occasion was made more special because Peter had not found it possible to lay it off. I went back to Ballydoyle and built more stables with the funds.

Peter has not only given his talents to the racecourse but deserves much praise for the work he has done towards the welfare of horses. In my time he must rank as one of the greatest figures in racing and I consider myself very fortunate to have had him as a friend.

One of the most famous and most successful associations of modern racing has been that between Vincent O'Brien and owner-breeder Robert Sangster, who has found Peter O'Sullevan an ally since his early racing days.

Robert Sangster

Peter was a great influence on me during my formative racing years, in my late twenties and early thirties. It was over dinner with him and the late John Hughes, then Clerk of the Course at Haydock Park, that the idea was born to stage a valuable sprint race at Haydock at the very end of the Flat season in which two-year-olds, who by then were not so far short of the three-year-olds in terms of maturity, could take on older horses. The race would be sponsored by my father's company Vernon's Pools – and thus the Vernons November Sprint Cup was born.

The first running, on 5 November 1966, immediately vindicated our idea, with Peter's two-year-old Be Friendly winning decisively from Green Park, owned by Charles Engelhard. That Be Friendly had won the inaugural running of the family race – and went on to win it again in 1967 before being thwarted by the fog in 1968 – drew my attention to the horse as a potential stallion, and by the time Be Friendly went to the Ennistown Stud in County Meath I had taken a quarter share in him, along with Peter himself, Stephen Raphael and trainer Jeremy Hindley. Be Friendly was my first ever interest in a stallion.

The other scheme which Peter and I dreamed up was the Tote Roll-Up, a weekly handicap with sixteen runners in which punters had to predict the first six home in the correct order. If the prize were not won, the pool would be carried over – or 'roll up' – to the following week. The Roll-Up began in April 1973 with around 400,000 entries, but Littlewoods declined to have the entry form on their coupon. Had they allowed this, rather than having a separate coupon, the scheme certainly would have worked.

In his quiet and retiring fashion, Peter has been very influential behind the scenes in racing, not least in the way he has brought people together. His opinion is so respected that some of the great racing partnerships have come about as a result of his having a quiet word in the right place: that is, for example, how Lester Piggott first came to ride for Vincent O'Brien, and Peter's considerable regard for the O'Brien skill was a factor in my own connection with Vincent.

Peter is a very great commentator – though I'm sure I can always tell what he's backed! – and the best professional racing man in the last thirty years. He knows every criminal and every good guy in the game, and probably should have been Senior Steward of the Jockey Club!

But the influence of Peter O'Sullevan has stretched well beyond the racecourse. Television presenter Katie Boyle, a tireless worker for animal charities including the Battersea Dogs' Home, offers a personal tribute.

Katie Boyle

My late husband Greville Baylis was mad about racing – his horse Richer won the Cambridgeshire in 1952 – and since we were neighbours of Peter and Pat in Chelsea in the late 1950s, the four of us came to be good friends, though my friendship with Peter did not then stretch to much heartfelt enthusiasm for the Turf. I'd go racing out of loyalty to Greville, but I really wasn't that interested: a mark of my attitude to the sport is that I'd conceal a copy of *Reader's Digest* or some other handily packaged reading material inside my racecard to keep myself amused as the afternoon wore on!

Had we been rich enough to have owned and run a stud, so that I could have watched the foals born, grow up and then race, it would have been a very different story. I just hated the idea of having to sell the horses and lose contact with them. Having long ago taken the side of animals in their fight against abuse and neglect at the hands of humans, I'd come to the conclusion that perhaps I didn't like racing because I cared too much about the horses. But when Greville bought me an advance Christmas present in the form of a yearling colt I started to get more involved, and as with most new racehorse owners the first piece of fun was finding the colt a name. I told Greville: 'You want him to be fast, I just want him to be friendly. So let's call him Fast And Friendly.'

The first time Fast And Friendly won, at Hurst Park in 1958, I was rushing off the stand to welcome him back when I saw the trainer Jeremy Tree.

'Isn't it wonderful? He's won! He's won!'

'Mmmm,' murmured Jeremy: 'He just beat mine.'

Then up came Peter, who was thrilled for us, and asked about how Fast And Friendly had come to be so named. When I told him, he vowed to call his own next horse Just Friendly – so I can claim a small footnote in racing history by being the source of the 'Friendly' in the names of so many of Peter's horses.

In the early days of my friendship with Peter I was, I have to admit, in awe of him. I tend to be over-exuberant; he's always been so private. I often felt that whatever I was saying to him was too much. Yet at the same time I was utterly fascinated by him, and (Pat won't mind my saying this) found him very attractive: I thought he looked just like my then ideal of glamorous manhood, the Shah of Persia!

My marriage to Greville was somewhat fiery, and Peter had the ability to walk a tightrope of friendship between us with great tact and humour. Then in 1976 I was suddenly and devastatingly widowed, and his compassion and understanding were beyond belief. Far from being remote, he proved himself a wonderful listener and a true tower of strength at a time of massive crisis in my life – a debt I'll never be able to repay. An immensely busy man, he was always generous with his time, and never made me feel rushed.

That same generosity with his time has applied to the extensive support he has – with characteristic quietness and diffidence – given to the charities for which we have joined forces. Unlike many others who lend their names to charities, Peter will get involved: he'll write letters, he'll make telephone calls, he'll attend demonstrations. He'll stand up and be counted.

Now happily married to another steadfast Peter – Peter Saunders – I find myself thinking of that passage in the New Testament when Christ tells the apostle: 'Thou art Peter, and upon this rock I will build my church.' The greatest tribute I can pay Peter O'Sullevan is that he has always been to me precisely that – a rock.

A mark of the O'Sullevan character was described in February 1997 in the William Hickey column in Peter's long-time writing home the Daily Express.

His courtesy is unrivalled. One evening recently, when an inebriated Munnoo approached him in his Chelsea apartment block and insisted on delivering his O'Sullevan imitation, Peter listened politely, complimented my man on his mimicry, wished him well in life and said: 'I hope I live long enough to one day impersonate you.' An eighteen-carat gent.

2

Calling the horses

THE PRESS ASSOCIATION, LIMITED.

RACING   JKG/JGB

P.O. BOX NO. 67
85, FLEET STREET,
LONDON, E.C.4.

TELEGRAPHIC ADDRESS:
"PRESS ASSOCIATION LONDON"
TELEPHONE: CENTRAL 7440
(21 LINES)

3rd Feb.1949

P. J. O'Sullevan, Esq.,
  14, Beverley House,
     Britten Street,
        London, S. W. 3.

Dear Mr. O'Sullevan,

         In reply to your letter of the 26th ultimo,

the Editor-in-Chief has given permission for you to assist

in the B.B. C., broadcast on the Grand National.

                  Yours sincerely,

                    Racing Editor.

That Peter O'Sullevan is so frequently described as 'The Voice of Racing' is testimony to his pre-eminence as a commentator; and, despite his achievements as a newspaper journalist, it is as a commentator that he is most revered and regarded.

Many writers have tried to get to grips with the essence of the O'Sullevan style. In The Racey Bits, *a book published in 1987 in aid of the Bob Champion Cancer Trust, Mark Siggers and Chris Williams explain:*

O'Sullevan's apparent ability to breathe only on alternate Tuesdays enables him to identify and recite the name of every horse in a thirty-strong Grand National field without the slightest pause or hesitation. Capable of phenomenal speed and volume, he is prone to medically dangerous excitement.

Contributors to this section anatomize the nature and demeanour of 'The Voice'.

Writing in the Sunday Telegraph *in October 1989, Russell Davies described the O'Sullevan voice as 'perhaps the only "hectic drawl" in captivity', and encapsulated the way those familiar tones are part of the background of so many lives.*

Russell Davies

Most of us who are not regular racegoers have picked up what little we know about horses from the television. It's a dangerous way to learn. What really rubs off on the armchair viewer is not a knowledge of the animals and their handlers and their pilots, but a patchy command of the racing lingo. Indeed, you can acquire a startling command of the trackside idiom without knowing the slightest thing about the game.

This was borne in upon me some years ago during a visit to my maternal grandmother, an amateur current affairs fanatic whose television was always on in hopes of a dramatic interruption from the News Room.

A stationmaster's widow in deepest Wales, she had, I can confidently state, never set foot on a racecourse or had the remotest social dealings with a turf accountant. Yet as the horses flashed past the post that afternoon, to the accompanying bluebottle-like hum of Peter O'Sullevan's commentary, the old lady suddenly announced, in a tone so aggrieved as to suggest that her life savings had gone down with the favourite, 'Lester Piggott never had a *smell*!' It was easily the most shocking phrase I ever heard her utter, though palpably justified by events.

I am disinclined to blame Mr O'Sullevan for filling the heads of old ladies with irrelevant phraseology. In fact I think he does a lot of good in this line. If one's afternoons are going to be filled by events in which one has no vital interest – emotional, intellectual or financial – then it is at least a pleasant bonus to have the doings of this alien world described by a person who really feels blessed to inhabit it. Mr O'Sullevan communicates this blessedness unfailingly, even though it stands to reason that some of the time he must be calling, through clenched teeth, winners who are doing his pocket no good . . .

In an article in the Sporting Life *in November 1996, Chris McGrath, in the course of an extensive profile of Peter O'Sullevan and an examination of the respect the whole sport pays to him, summed up the effect of his commentating life.*

Chris McGrath

It was the great achievement of O'Sullevan, and the other broadcasting icons of his vintage, to resolve this paradox: the impersonal modern scale of something so personally emotional as sport. Far from just calling the horses, O'Sullevan put the emotion into their motion – their miraculous, miniature motion before the sofas of ordinary people all over Britain. Like his nearest rival in terms of endurance, Bill McLaren (started five years later, in 1952), O'Sullevan has woven together the manifold strands of our personal experience to produce a communal memory.

If you go to a rainswept rugby international at Murrayfield, you have the experience unbeatably in the raw. But you still tape the game, so that you can watch it again with Bill. In the same way, O'Sullevan did not simply convey what he – but not you – could see in the flesh. He created a parallel, no less legitimate, experience. Friends with no particular interest in racing rehearse, word for word, which of Desert Orchid and Yahoo was on the far side, which on the near side; can time and again absorb the drama of the Irish mare 'beginning to get up'.

So what was the special way in which O'Sullevan bridged that gap, between the steaming beasts tearing clods out of a Cotswold hill and a million suburban lives? His technical assets were obvious: the voice, which is not glibly mellifluous but has a hint of austerity; that voice's instant obedience, for so many years, to an eye that missed nothing; and its use of words tailored exactly to the action (none of your off-the-peg 'scraping paint'-type phrases) . . .

The Timeform Organization, in the entry on Peter O'Sullevan's horse Attivo in Chasers & Hurdlers 1975–76, *drew historical comparisons to illustrate the O'Sullevan quality.*

Timeform

Some may think our horses are not all they used to be; others may say our jockeys are not a patch on some of those in former times. But there's no getting away from one thing: our commentators are miles ahead of the old school. Nobody who has tried to read a race from start to finish needs telling what a difficult task it is, and most of today's television and radio commentators do an excellent job. Peter O'Sullevan, Attivo's owner, has set the standard of race-reading that is now a model for all other commentators. Accurate, coherent, impartial, he's the complete professional. There's no time-wasting, no hesitation, no needless repetition and although his speech is rapid – we have timed him at 240 words a minute – every word is clear. Here's O'Sullevan's description of the last half-mile of Nijinsky's Derby, a typical example of his work:

> As they run round Tattenham Corner it's Long Till in the lead from Cry Baby, then Mon Plaisir, then Meadowville; Gyr's towards the outside, Nijinsky towards the inner. As they race round the home turn now and it's Long Till, Meadowville, then comes Mon Plaisir, Gyr with his white face showing towards the outside. As they come to the three-furlong marker it's Meadowville in the centre with Long Till on the far side and Gyr coming there very strongly. Great Wall has burst through over on the far side. Stintino is making a run towards the near side. And it's Great Wall under pressure from Gyr. Gyr now has taken it up at the two-furlong pole, it's Gyr under pressure in the lead being pressed by Great Wall. Then comes Nijinsky. Then Stintino. They're racing up towards the furlong marker and here comes Lester Piggott on Nijinsky. It's Gyr on the far side, Lester Piggott on the near side on Nijinsky. Nijinsky coming to take it up from Gyr and racing up towards the line it's a fifth for

Lester Piggott. Nijinsky's gone clear. Nijinsky the winner, Gyr second, Stintino is third. Fourth is Great Wall and five Meadowville. Sixth is The Swell and seven Approval and eight Long Till. Nine is Cry Baby and ten is Tambourine Man and eleventh and last is Mon Plaisir.

Now let's take up from the same stage of the race the commentary by Raymond Glendenning on the 1948 Derby. This was one of Glendenning's best efforts, yet it's hardly in the same street as O'Sullevan's:

I can't see anything to beat Royal Drake at the moment. Straight Play is there, coming up there. It's Royal Drake, with Djeddah there. A furlong and a half to go; Royal Drake is three lengths clear and it looks to me another victory for France. My Babu is coming very hard on the outside. So is My Love, and it's My Love coming up to challenge him now. It's now Royal Drake half a length ahead with a hundred yards to go. My Love's coming up now. My Love is beating him with fifty yards to go, and he's a length ahead. Twenty-five yards, and at the post My Love wins, Royal Drake second, Noor third.

Glendenning's effusive style and his awareness only of the leaders in a race earned him many detractors. But even those who complained most bitterly about Glendenning would readily admit that his description of the finish of the 1948 Derby compares very well indeed with the radio commentary on the 1933 race given by Bob Lyle, distinguished racing correspondent of *The Times*. This was Hyperion's year and there were twenty-four runners. You'd hardly think it from the commentary. Here it is, again from four furlongs out:

I can't see the horses at the moment. I can see Lord Derby, though, looking very pleased; his are first and second. Hyperion has the rails, looks like winning it too. He'll be first and second, Lord Derby. King Salmon is coming. Hyperion wins it, the horse with the form; then King Salmon. Wins it by lengths and lengths; won easy in a canter, no doubt about that. I could have given it when they came into the straight. Isn't it wonderful? And you can't see it at all. The judge extraordinarily agrees with me; he puts Hyperion first, then King Salmon.

One of O'Sullevan's strong points is that he keeps the emotion down to the minimum. Even when a horse of his own is concerned in an exciting finish he manages to remain calm. When Attivo won the 1974 Daily Express Triumph Hurdle, the most important race over the sticks for four-year-olds, O'Sullevan's commentary on the race for the BBC betrayed no trace of partiality or feeling. In the same year O'Sullevan had to commentate on another race for which Attivo was a fancied contender, the Ladbroke Chester Cup, one of the richest long-distance handicaps on the Flat. Attivo got home by a short head after a ding-dong battle with Kambalda in the last furlong; O'Sullevan, as usual, was imperturbable.

Monty Court, former editor of the Sporting Life *and a long-time friend and admirer of Peter O'Sullevan, also cites Attivo's Chester Cup when applauding his calmness under pressure.*

Monty Court

One of the great gifts enjoyed by all outstanding public performers is the talent to behave like a swan – the ability to present a picture of sublime serenity on the surface in spite of the fact that they might be paddling like hell underneath. It's the talent that makes moments of extreme pressure appear facile and simple. And Peter O'Sullevan has been doing it all his broadcasting life.

This remarkable veteran of BBC Sport has been helped, of course, by a velvet-smooth voice, with the result that for the best part of half a century viewers have been treated to clear, non-hysterical commentaries of silky smoothness in the face of onrushing charges of thirty and more sprinters that would induce mental collapse and vocal seizure in lesser mortals. There's no chance of copping out in those seconds when the massive fields for Royal Ascot's Wokingham Stakes or Royal Hunt Cup fan out in their charge to the line, or in the final stages of Glorious Goodwood's Stewards' Cup.

Like all good professionals, O'Sullevan has always worked hard to make it look easy, as many colleagues will testify having seen him grey-faced after hours of study of unfamiliar names and colours in preparation for foreign races or hunter-chases. But his calmness under pressure has surprised even those who thought they knew him best.

In his retirement apartment in Majorca, veteran trainer Cyril Mitchell still talks with awe of the most exciting moment in O'Sullevan's racing life – the day, more than thirty years ago, when Be Friendly won the first running of the Vernons November Sprint Cup at Haydock Park. This was the moment when the O'Sullevan two-year-old took on the greatest sprinters in the land – and in the biggest field ever to line up for the race. Mitchell was allowed to watch the race from the BBC commentary box perched high on scaffolding over the Tattersalls enclosure, and watched Be Friendly's pre-planned manoeuvre work like a dream as he was brought across to the stand rails to win the then considerable prize of £5,337 by two lengths.

It was an immense thrill that sent a surge of exhilaration through the system of even the normally ice-cool Mitchell, but all he was aware of was the calm, measured voice of O'Sullevan going through his usual post-race routine and telling viewers: 'First Be Friendly, owned by Peter O'Sullevan, trained by Cyril Mitchell and ridden by Colin Williams . . .' Mitchell struggled to come to terms with the thrill that he knew O'Sullevan was experiencing and the composed voice that might have been reading out something as mundane as a shopping list. Was this really the voice of the man who had agonized about putting up an apprentice who couldn't claim his allowance in such a valuable race? Was this really the voice of a man who was so anxious before the race that he walked the course twice? Was this the voice of a man who had shrugged off jibes about the horse not having even the remotest chance and who had napped it against all the odds in his *Daily Express* column – and backed it at 10–1?

'It was quite unreal,' recalls Mitch. 'I shall never forget it because I know how excited he was. Let's face it – it was a hell of a day, a hell of a thrill. He even waved to the punters below, who were shouting and cheering up at him. But he never lost his cool with his commentary. There were a lot of other big days with the horse, but I shall never forget that one.'

The O'Sullevan calmness under fire also impressed the party watching the race in Sandown's Royal Box (and they know a thing or two about hiding their feelings!), and Sir Martin Gilliat, the Queen Mother's secretary, wrote in a letter: 'We in the box at Sandown were all filled with admiration for your "apparent" ice-cool outlook when doing the commentary. Queen Elizabeth has asked me to let you know how delighted she was and sends her warmest congratulations.'

This same calmness at moments which might make other men hysterical has never failed to impress John Hanmer, who has shared his BBC commentary box for twenty-five years. The admiration that Hanmer felt over the man's demeanour when Attivo won the Triumph Hurdle was boosted even further in the commentary on the Chester Cup when

Attivo beat Kambalda by the shortest of short heads – and further still
when a gale blew the door off the Chepstow commentary box in mid-
race but still failed to check the O'Sullevan flow.

Like all masters of his profession, O'Sullevan became a yardstick
against which all aspiring newcomers were measured, and this certainly
helped curb some of their clichéd excesses. Now that he is preparing to
go, rising eighty, we must prepare ourselves for a new wave. I can only
repeat something I wrote in one of my *Sporting Life* columns: 'Maybe we
will then realize that we lost not only a voice but an art as well.'

As senior race-caller for Channel Four, Graham Goode has taken over Peter O'Sullevan's role as television commentator for Cheltenham. He acknowledges his debt to the master.

Graham Goode

We all tend to overlook the fact that television coverage of sport is relatively new. I always used to watch *Grandstand* and during the school holidays Goodwood and Ascot, Cheltenham and Aintree. Through the years as I listened to Peter O'Sullevan on the television I used to think to myself, I could do that – and I am! That has got to be one million to one and no tax.

Peter O'Sullevan was, along with Brian Johnston, Dan Maskell, Peter West, Peter Dimmock, Henry Longhurst, Ken Wolstenholme, Eddie Waring and David Coleman, one of the founding fathers of television commentating. He set the standard by which all aspiring racing commentators were judged and has carried that torch for fifty years: a truly remarkable *tour de force*.

As the family were not only racing fans, but *Daily Express* readers, we all but sent a Christmas card to Bert at the garage. Peter inevitably brought the reader the news he wanted to read; I wonder how many journalists he likewise inspired.

Simon Holt, who began commentating on racecourses in 1988 and joined Channel Four Racing in 1994, represents the younger generation of commentators who have taken inspiration from Peter O'Sullevan.

Simon Holt

No horse and no jockey has had a greater influence on my career in racing than Peter O'Sullevan – and he would probably be too modest to realize! Like so many of us, I grew up with his television commentaries and they have provided fatherly guidance, reference and inspiration for my own rather less worthy efforts. Only a few great commentators can actually enhance the sporting moments they describe, and lay claim to that indefinable, unquantifiable broadcasting skill: gravitas. Henry Longhurst, Dan Maskell, John Arlott and Harry Carpenter might have had a drop or two of the golden gift – but O'Sullevan had gravitas by the gallon.

Some of Peter's commentaries are as memorable as the races; his words, and their weighty, authoritative delivery in that perfectly pitched voice – a voice made for a horse race – will never be forgotten. Red Rum's first Grand National: 'And Crisp is getting very tired, he's wandering off a true line, he's been out there on his own for a long time'; and (some yards from the line with Crisp still in front): 'Red Rum's finishing the stronger, Red Rum's going to win the National.' Surely one of the greatest of horse races complemented by a commentator who neither embellished nor understated but who didn't waste the moment. There are many others, space only to name a few. The Grundy–Bustino battle in the King George: 'And Bustino's fighting back . . .'; Red Rum's third Grand National: 'You've never heard a reception like it at Liverpool, Red Rum wins the National!'; Dawn Run's Gold Cup: 'The mare's beginning to get up . . .'; Sea Pigeon in the Champion Hurdle: 'It's the old man, Sea Pigeon, coming to take it up . . .' These are lines which have marked the course of racing history.

Surprising, perhaps, but I hardly know Peter at all. I think he is probably quite a private man; there is a big age difference between us and (unusual for a race-caller) I tend to become a little tongue-tied in his company. It is a measure of the respect I have for him.

It has been an extraordinary career, first and foremost for the unfailing accuracy and excellence of performance, but also for his knowledge, class and, like the greatest of stayers, his endurance. He has run a remarkable race. Calling the horses (to borrow the title of his autobiography) ought to be a young man's game – it requires mental alertness, a good memory and sharp eyesight – but, unlike most racehorses who have become a bit long in the tooth, 'the old man' has, for half a century, pulled out sound on race day, ready to produce his best. Peter O'Sullevan will always be the nation's favourite, and if this selling-plater (already in need of a pair of blinkers on occasions) can keep going for half as long, and rate half as highly, it will be a considerable turn up for the books.

In this extract adapted from his racing autobiography Die Broke, *Jamie Reid – one of the most acute contemporary observers of the racing scene – expresses his own debt to Peter O'Sullevan.*

Jamie Reid

My earliest memories of Cheltenham races are of watching the 1961 National Hunt Festival on television at home in Leigh in West Kent. I was two months short of my seventh birthday and I had just been awarded an unexpected two-week holiday from primary school as a result of going down with mumps. My gambling-mad grandmother, who was herself eighty-four at the time, had already introduced me to the louche pleasures of horse racing. On the Monday evening she rang up to say that there was something rather special on television over the next three days. I should watch it. I'd remember it. I did watch; and it's no exaggeration to say that the impression it made on me has pretty much dictated the course of my entire life.

When I look back now to those events of more than three decades ago, I remember inspirational horses like the Gold Cup winner Saffron Tartan and the Champion Hurdler, Eborneezer. I remember their charismatic jockeys and trainers like Fred Winter and Captain Ryan Price. And I think of the vivid black and white pictures of the far-flung racecourse and its stirring backdrop. But what really made that first Cheltenham for me, and what was to make every other Festival and every racing experience for years to come, was the matchless commentary of Peter O'Sullevan.

Like all the truly great broadcasters, be it on sport, politics, the arts or whatever, O'Sullevan has always combined a deep and profound love of and knowledge of his subject with a fluent and imaginative grasp of language. That inimitable and distinctive voice with its rich timbre and mellifluous tone – so far from nasal Estuary English on the one hand or blocked-nose County on the other – was classic and classy but never affected or excluding. O'Sullevan's commentaries patronized no one and included everyone from the wealthiest Jockey Club grandee to the

61

simplest armchair punter. He was one of the first men to democratize a sport in this way. But he was also a rigorous professional. And someone who understood that television is primarily a visual medium and that the success of any transmission depends partly on the quality and smoothness of the visual images and partly on the authority of the commentator. Words should be used sparingly but to telling effect. O'Sullevan's courteous though fundamentally shy personality infuses his work but doesn't overwhelm it. He has never been a man merely to gabble names frantically or to cheapen round the edges. His economy of style, just as much as his grasp of high drama, underlines that if you want to get close to the beauty and magic of horse racing you mustn't spread it too thin or the outcome will be merely hackneyed and banal. For the big moments to count there must be rationing, and you can't start drumming up bogus excitement about routine races on uneventful afternoons.

O'Sullevan couldn't possibly know the result of a horse race in advance any more than those of us watching and listening with him. But what he could do, and what connected with me powerfully from the age of seven onwards, was unfold his commentaries like a story. An enthrallingly classical story with a proper beginning, middle and end. A story brimming with suspense and punctuated by its own decisive moments of victory and defeat, triumph and despair.

I think what I sensed as long ago as 1961 was that something about the very nature of Cheltenham racecourse enhanced and enriched every story set there. That long opening run up past the stands was the bright and positive beginning, the point at which every character's hopes and expectations were still intact. Then would come the sweep out into the country, followed by the stamina-sapping climb on the far side of the track; the top of the hill; the accelerating downhill chase; the left-handed turn into the straight; the final few fences as the noise of the crowd got louder and, for the horses, closer and more distracting and more intense – and then that climactic uphill run to the death.

These natural breaks and contours provided the perfect structure for O'Sullevan's narratives. They were his chapter headings and paragraphs, his commas and full stops. And if you knew what to look for and how to read and translate the changing tones and inflections in his voice, you would often find that he seemed to know or spot what the principals were doing or were about to do just before they did it. Who would play their big cards when and how, and who would play their best cards first? Who would go too soon and tie up? Who would sit waiting in behind? Who would try and hold on to their lead from beginning to end? And who would come late and trump the pack?

O'Sullevan's love of horses and his respect for their courage and gameness have been well documented. But he also cherished flair and élan. And, as I began to understand as I got older and started to bet and race regularly, he had the greatest respect for the consummate professionals. The jockeys and trainers – and the bookies and punters – who could step up a gear on the big occasion. A gambled-on Irish novice at Cheltenham. A crack French three-year-old on the Flat. Francome. O'Neill. Yves Saint-Martin. Lester Piggott. Vincent O'Brien. They were his type, and it was for them that he reserved his highest praise.

I have no complaints about the technical quality of Channel Four's coverage of the Festival. They have brought with them many exciting new camera angles as well as other refreshing innovations. But for all the enthusiasm of their commentary team, Cheltenham just isn't the same without O'Sullevan behind the microphone. There have been so many unforgettable moments over the past thirty-six years. Races and commentaries so replete with poetry and emotion that they still make the hairs stand up on the back of my neck. Pas Seul and Saffron Tartan. Mandarin and Fortria. What A Myth. Stalbridge Colonist. Kirriemuir. Persian War. Bula. Comedy of Errors. Pendil and The Dikler and Captain Christy. Night Nurse, Monksfield and Sea Pigeon. Noddy's Ryde and Bobsline. Golden Cygnet. Attivo. Mister Donovan. Forgive'N Forget. Silver Buck and Bregawn. Brown Chamberlin and Burrough Hill Lad. Ten Plus. Desert Orchid. The Fellow. Dawn Run. Arkle and Mill House. 'And Pat Taaffe being shouted for from the stands now. Irish voices really beginning to call for him as he starts to make up ground . . .'

For myself, and I know for thousands of others like me, Peter O'Sullevan was and always will be *the voice* of racing, *non pareil*.

When at the end of 1994 the BBC relinquished coverage of Cheltenham to Channel Four Racing, one of the great characters of the jumping game was quick to pen a note of appreciation to the man who had called home her two Gold Cup winners – Burrough Hill Lad in 1984 and Garrison Savannah, who got home by a short head from The Fellow in 1991.

Jenny Pitman

It is with sadness that I read in today's papers that it will be your last day commentating at Cheltenham.

The end of another era! Apart from nearly causing my premature death in the '91 Gold Cup, we have always enjoyed your commentaries. The professionalism that you have shown over the years, without gimmicks and self-praise, has made you the most outstanding 'caller of horses' ever, and I very much doubt your natural ability will be matched in future years.

I do hope that you have an enjoyable day, and that Cheltenham and the BBC provide you with some suitable refreshment to quench what I am sure will be a very dry throat by the end of your commentary today.

A wet day at Newmarket. Picture Post/Haywood Magee

Race-reading with Peter Dimmock.

At Laurel for the Washington DC International, 1958.

Lunching with Pat at the Château de Madrid, Villefranche-sur-Mer, 1954.

Paul Louis, Nice

Commentating on the first computerized horse race, a stand-in for the abandoned 1967 Massey-Ferguson Gold Cup; Julian Wilson lends a hand. The 'winner' was 6-1 chance Arctic Sunset. United Press International

Be Friendly: (above) with admiring owner after the Vernons November Sprint Cup at Haydock Park, 1967; and (below) going to post with Scobie Breasley before the Nunthorpe Stakes at York, 1968. Alec Russell (above) & Daily Express

On his last day as a jockey, Fred Winter on Friendly Again (sheepskin noseband) is collared by Mishgar (Owen McNally) in the Clive Graham Handicap Hurdle, Cheltenham, 1964. Daily Express

Attivo (Robert Hughes) makes a mess of the final flight but goes on to land the Daily Express Triumph Hurdle, Cheltenham, 1974. Sport & General Press Agency

At the launch of Calling the Horses*: (above) with, left to right, Jimmy Lindley, Scobie Breasley, Geoff Lewis, Joe Mercer, Brough Scott, Edward Hide, Lester Piggott and Peter Scudamore; and (below) John McCririck.* Alan F. Raymond

Paperwork: (above) going through the post with long-suffering secretary Valerie Frost after Be Friendly's victory in the inaugural Vernons November Sprint Cup, 1966; and (below) with 'The Scout', Clive Graham. Daily Express

Daily Express

Henry Kelly, an enthusiastic racing man when his extensive commitments to radio and television allow, has long been in the vanguard of the Peter O'Sullevan Fan Club. Writing of the week's sport on television in The Times *just after the 1992 Grand National, he homed in on another O'Sullevan characteristic: the knack, whatever the occasion, to say just what needs to be said.*

Henry Kelly

Let us now praise famous men: those brave ones who ride horses over fences at breakneck speed so that the rest of us – too wise or too afraid to do it ourselves – can have a day out in the country, lots of fun and games, and maybe make a bob or two.

I have either listened to, watched or been at the Aintree Grand National ever since I was a child. Yet each year, no matter how blasé I might get beforehand, when the horses are wheeling around at the start of this wonderful race I still get a nerve-tingling sense of excitement out of all proportion with anything in sport I could ever have experienced personally.

This year the BBC's coverage included cameras hidden in fences. Wisely, they left these shots until the replay. To be honest, they didn't add much to the enjoyment of the race. What was remarkable were the cameras in the back of the boats during the Boat Race and the ones used by the Beeb from the side of some of the fences at Aintree.

As usual, the BBC's coverage – with the exception of the ludicrous idea of having music under the introduction of the National horses – was first-class. But let us praise one famous man above them all: Peter O'Sullevan. He is a different class, isn't he, O'Sullevan? Word-perfect, calm when needs be, and the modulated tones rising to a tremor of excitement just when needed. He does no more and no less than he should. He walks and talks like a man assuring us that everything is going to be all right.

If he never said another word, did he not perfectly sum up the feelings of so many people in racing on Saturday? During the final stages of the Aintree Martell Hurdle, O'Sullevan found himself calling home Morley

Street, winning the race for the third time in a row, a fabulous achievement. Morley Street is owned by Michael Jackson, a millionaire paper-selling racing enthusiast. Until Saturday Morley Street was always ridden by Jimmy Frost, the popular West Country rider, who won something in the region of £400,000 on him for Jackson. Morley Street was beaten last month when ridden by Frost. Jackson sacked the rider. At Aintree on Saturday the new rider, Richard Dunwoody, won the race, by a whisker. As they flashed past the post, O'Sullevan said: 'And Morley Street wins the race, but he wins it like a shadow of his former self. No wonder Jimmy Frost didn't win the Champion Hurdle on him.' Just what needed to be said: nothing more, nothing less. End message.

For many years Desmond Lynam has worked with Peter O'Sullevan on BBC coverage of the Grand National. One day stands out.

Desmond Lynam

Over the years the BBC has had the knack of finding – in all sorts of areas, but especially in sport – broadcasters of extraordinary stature, and Peter O'Sullevan is certainly one of them. I've worked with many of the top sports commentators over the years, on both radio and television, but there is nobody in the business that I admire more than Peter. His talent, his approach to his work, his dedication and his status within his sport – all are outstanding. And alongside those professional attributes, he's a gentleman of the old school: charming, a little shy, modest about his standing.

Calling the horses seems to me significantly different from all other forms of sports commentary – that instantaneous transference of thought from colours to name as forty horses come flashing past – and I'm amazed by how people can do it, and by how Peter can still do it better than anyone has ever done it. He has a mind that can cope with the demands of very quick thinking, and most of all he is blessed in his instrument, that voice: nobody has ever had a voice quite like it, with that unique, instantly recognizable resonance and pitch.

From the first time I fronted the Grand National coverage for television in 1985 – the year of Last Suspect – I've found Peter a delight to work with. Some experts within sport can be over-protective of their speciality, but Peter is always open, always willing to share his knowledge; and, in addition to being a top race-reader, he is a journalist with an unerring feel for a story, as was apparent during what was probably the most famous – certainly the most notorious – outside broadcast we worked on together, the 1993 Grand National.

As the runners circled at the start I was in my position in the Aintree unsaddling enclosure, from where I would interview winning connections immediately after the race. I was watching the race on the monitor there, and when the first false start took place realized that a pretty big story was unfolding: how would they get the field back to try again? But get them back they did, only for the second false start and the fiasco of all but nine of the runners setting off towards the first fence. 'Now we've got chaos on our hands!', I thought, but Peter's professionalism at that moment of crisis for his sport helped put the shenanigans into context.

That day separate directors were handling Peter's commentary and my own presentation, so I could not hear through my earpiece his initial reaction, other than what I was getting from the actual transmission. In any event, there was very little talkback coming over as the drama unfolded: most people were too stunned to talk!

Throughout his commentary Peter kept painting the broad picture, kept reminding viewers that although they were watching horses running, and he was identifying who those horses were, it was meaningless as a contest and would not count. His words as the leaders crossed the line – 'and so Esha Ness wins the Grand National that never was' – formed the perfect phrase for that moment.

In the chaotic aftermath, Peter continued to be the voice of reason. He knew that what had happened was not a disaster – it was, after all, simply a huge cock-up – and during our post-race interview his calm, rounded view helped me put the whole bizarre afternoon into perspective.

No doubt about it: Peter is one of the legends and I'm privileged to count him a friend.

Another of the great names of sports broadcasting to have worked alongside Peter O'Sullevan is Peter Dimmock, described in Calling the Horses *as having made 'the most significant contribution to outside broadcasting of his era'. In the late 1940s, before reaching the heights of the BBC as producer, presenter and executive, Peter Dimmock had a spell as a racing commentator for both radio and television.*

Peter Dimmock

I first met Peter O'Sullevan when I joined the Racing Department of the Press Association after being demobilized as a pilot in the Royal Air Force and a staff officer at the Air Ministry. We sat opposite one another at the racing desk under the watchful eye of Mr Harrison, who was a stickler for good grammar and hard work! We always hoped to be sent to race meetings – at the heart of the action, as it were.

When I joined BBC Television's Outside Broadcasts department I was asked to undertake race commentaries when Frank More O'Ferrall was ill. As this was in addition to my administrative work, they did not have to pay me, on the basis of 'SNF' – 'Staff No Fee'.

To begin with I had a race-reader, and then invited Peter to assist me, as a PA colleague who regularly went racing. I could only manage the odd meeting, and Peter quickly absorbed the technique of race commentating with me, on both radio and television. As I became more heavily involved as both an administrator and a producer of BBC TV Outside Broadcasts, I had to forgo race commentary and handed over to Peter, who never ceased to grumble about the inadequacies of our equipment in those post-war days – and still does!

With 1,678 winners over jumps in Britain to his credit, Peter Scudamore is the most successful jockey in the history of National Hunt racing. After quitting the saddle in 1993 he embarked on a career in journalism and broadcasting, and in the latter area has been working for the BBC alongside Peter O'Sullevan. As news of the impending retirement sank in, Peter Scudamore offered this appreciation in his Daily Mail *column in November 1996.*

Peter Scudamore

Working with Peter O'Sullevan is awe-inspiring. When he retires, his name in racing will be uttered in the same breath as other true greats of our sport such as Vincent O'Brien, Lester Piggott and Fred Winter. He has been given that place because of the respect he has earned from the racing fraternity as a brilliant commentator and journalist. His clear, accurate commentaries have unfolded the events of many of our major races for as long as I can remember. As a jockey, a major race was given an extra significance for me if he was calling it. Changing from the saddle to the microphone made me realize that talking on television was not as easy as O'Sullevan's commanding manner makes it seem. Honoured with the title of the 'Voice of Racing', it is easy to take for granted O'Sullevan's accuracy, but a glance behind the scenes reveals the hard work involved. Very often BBC racing is given a limited amount of time during *Grandstand*, but O'Sullevan's concise appraisals of the trainers, jockeys and horses concerned in the finishes brings home his deep knowledge of and feeling for the sport.

My riding was not always beyond criticism from O'Sullevan, either. He was particularly fault-finding of a race that I won on Bajan Sunshine at Haydock. He saw that my use of the whip was unacceptable. O'Sullevan has always been a great campaigner for the International League for the Protection of Horses, and judgement coming from someone for whom I had so much respect made me endeavour to change my use of the stick.

For most of the time that Peter O'Sullevan was dominating racing commentary on television, the equivalent role on radio was held by Peter Bromley – who early in his own BBC career was promised by Peter Dimmock that he would be in line to take over as senior racing commentator on television when Peter O'Sullevan retired. As he says now: 'Some apprenticeship!'

Peter Bromley

When I first came into racing as an impecunious amateur rider in the fifties, the *Daily Express* was the leading national paper for racing, with Clive Graham (The Scout) and Peter O'Sullevan's well-informed column essential reading for the followers of the sport. By the time I joined the BBC in 1959, these two were the commentators for BBC Television's coverage of racing, which in those golden days provided the centrepiece for *Grandstand*, Clive doing the paddock and Peter the race. I became the 'third man', covering for either of them if their paper would not release them and later, when it was allowed, reporting on the betting and doing the interviews.

I spent many days alongside Peter in his windswept perches – some of those early commentaries were done from temporary scaffolding towers – providing him with the all-important 'U-SAID' cards confirming what he had actually called home and listening out for the public address announcement if there was a photo finish. I soon became aware that I was in the presence of a master of his craft and one of the great communicators in the new field of televised sport. I admired his restraint, his complete command of the spoken word. The phrase *le mot juste* could have been invented with Peter in mind. His voice carried authority, the context was conveyed concisely, and every word was delivered with a fluency and accuracy that were a marvel to witness at close hand.

When Raymond Glendenning retired from commentating on horse racing I was switched to radio to take over from him. So for the last thirty-eight years on BBC racecourses I have worked in the next-door box to Peter, covering the same races but for a very different audience.

The presentation of racing on television has changed a great deal since the early days. There was a time when Clive Graham, after a leisurely trawl through the runners in the paddock, handed over to Peter when the field came on to the course. Peter then had to carry commentary right through to the end of the race; yet no matter how long the delay at the start, Peter's ability to inform never flagged. This flow of information was possible only because he had used every available hour to prepare meticulously for each race. Racing is fortunate to have had such a dedicated and knowledgeable man to guide the television audience all these years. The deepest impressions I have formed have been of his abiding love of the sport and his absolute respect for the professionals who provide the action, the jockeys and trainers; and I have always admired the way he has so sympathetically handled the tragedy that sometimes goes hand in hand with success.

Throughout all these years his greatest concern has always been for the horses, those he has owned and the many millions he must have called. So, as this caring commentator starts to clock up the magic numbers – fifty Grand Nationals – make the most of the countdown to the final commentary and enjoy that distinctive voice taking you through the race, for his like do not pass through very often.

Australian journalist J. A. – Jim – McGrath gave his first commentary for the BBC in November 1992, and became part of the BBC's Grand National commentary team the following year.

J. A. McGrath

Peter O'Sullevan had just completed the first stage of the most worrying period in his commentating career. In the summer of 1993, at seventy-five years of age, he had decided to go ahead with the advice of an eye specialist, who recommended a double cataract operation.

Commentating on horse racing – or calling the horses, as Peter often terms it – is unlike commentating on any other sport for television or radio. It is a skill that relies heavily on short-term memory and almost entirely on instant identification, whether the horses happen to be in front of the stands or on the far side of the course. When the contestants are the best part of a mile away, and maybe running straight towards the commentator, perched high in the stand, the easiest way to identify them is to remember the different coloured jackets worn by the jockeys.

If there is one thing a good commentator needs, it is a good pair of eyes. After tests, Peter had been informed by the specialist that his eyes were operating at 40 per cent below 'normal'. Not unaccustomed to taking an educated punt at the best of times, Peter decided this was one gamble he had to take – and one that had to get up.

The O'Sullevan eye ops were one of racing's best-kept secrets. 'I was worried a bit beforehand, but knew I had to seek the best medical attention after calling that year's Irish Derby. I found myself busking at one stage of the race,' he told me. The cloak of secrecy that covered the operations was successfully held in place until Peter went to step into a taxi outside the Cromwell Hospital for the short ride to his Chelsea apartment. Despite a huge white eye-patch and his familiar trilby being pulled down at a more exaggerated angle than usual, he was instantly recognized. Inevitably, it was the London cabbie who cracked the case. 'Don't reckon you'll be seeing them too well this weekend, Pete,' he boldly suggested to his famous passenger. There followed a slightly awkward pause of five seconds or so. Thinking he might have overstepped the mark, he quickly added, 'but then, you'd only need one eye to be twice as good as the others, anyway.'

The eye ops were an amazing success. Peter could not believe the difference when it came to identifying the multicoloured jackets. 'The blue of Hamdan Al Maktoum's colours was so bright when I did my next meeting at Newbury that it dazzled me,' he later recalled.

Wherever and whenever the greats of sports commentating are mentioned, Peter O'Sullevan will be at the head of the list – or pretty near the top. Commentating on horse racing is far more complex than on other sports, such as tennis (two, or at most four, runners), golf (played over a period of hours and days) or motor racing (often repetitious after the leaders have been sorted out). The horses – and there are often over thirty of them – are moving very quickly, and a race such as the six-furlong Stewards' Cup at Goodwood can be over in seventy-five seconds or less. That Peter has been able to lead his field for fifty years is as much a tribute to his ability to adapt to trends and shape his commentary style accordingly as it is to his expertise and knowledge.

Personally, it was a memorable thrill in my much shorter commentating career to work alongside Peter for the first time at Longchamp in 1995. His preparation, technique and pure professionalism were wonderful to witness first-hand, and are features of his style and approach that I will never forget.

3

Scoop! Scoop! Scoop! Scoop!

Peter O'Sullevan the journalist

Peter O'Sullevan joined the Press Association as racing correspondent in 1944, and in 1950 moved to the Daily Express, *where he remained until 1986. His partnership with Clive Graham, who died in 1974, was the most potent and influential in post-war racing journalism. Revered as he may have been as a race commentator, for many admirers his journalism was of no less significance.*

Bob Findlay was sports editor of the Daily Express *for eight years during the period that Peter O'Sullevan worked there.*

Bob Findlay

In 1950 Clive Graham was promoted to the role of The Scout – chief racing writer on the *Daily Express*. The question was, who was to succeed him as gossip writer? Clive suggested Peter O'Sullevan, then an up-and-coming lad in the Press Association racing 'nursery' and a buddy of his. There followed an interview with Arthur Christiansen, the editor who took the *Express* to the four-and-a-half-million mark. Peter considered that £30 a week plus modest expenses was a good deal. The snag was broadcasting. Lord Beaverbrook saw it as the enemy, and frowned on his staff taking part. However, 'Chris' persuaded his lordship to allow Peter to do an 'occasional broadcast' so long as he first sought permission. Peter soon proved that the BBC and the *Express* could benefit mutually from his rising reputation in the racing world.

Peter stamped his own ethics on the job right from the start: no changes in his copy without consultation; no garish headlines; and no exploitation of his copy by the news desk whereby they could extract some titbit from his column to give them a front page story. This last inhibition drove us mad. Sometimes Peter would bury an item worthy of the front page deep in his column and, when asked if the news desk could have it, would reply: 'No way!' – perhaps because he might embarrass his contact by sensational exposure.

Peter's exclusives or scoops were too numerous to mention: the Rae Johnstone story is just one example. Rae Johnstone, the great Australian jockey, beckoned to Peter to come into the weighing room one day at Longchamp and said: 'This is my last ride, Peter.' It was as if the King had abdicated. And we made the most of it! An explosive blurb on the back page screamed:

Scoop! Peter O'Sullevan gave first news yesterday that Rae Johnstone had decided to retire!

Scoop! Peter O'Sullevan landed a 9–2 nap when Penultimate won the last race at Brighton.

Scoop! Peter O'Sullevan is £26 up on his naps this season.

Scoop! Peter O'Sullevan is showing a substantial profit on his naps for the seventh season out of eight!

Well, we did lay it on a bit thick, but wasn't it worth it? It certainly gave apoplexy to the editors of lesser newspapers. Of Peter's book, *The Rae Johnstone Story* – a sell-out – Chris commented: 'It is so coherent, so beautifully simple in its grace and style, that only Peter O'Sullevan could have written it.' Chris wrote a 'Bulletin' on the *Express* notice board each day handing out high praise or biting criticism to staff on that day's paper. Accolades for Peter were as plentiful as his scoops or winning naps.

Peter offered three tips a day in his column, including his nap. Its success was phenomenal. And though his tips were not strong on outsiders, his policy of 'small profits, quick returns' brought smiles to the faces of discerning punters. Tipping is a full-time job in itself, burning the midnight oil studying the form; writing a column in addition is a herculean task; add broadcasting, and only Peter could have done it.

Peter continued with the *Express* long after I had joined the *Daily Sketch*, but some years later, as sports editor, I had the pleasure of writing to him after Be Friendly's first triumph in the Vernons at Haydock Park: 'What are you trying to do – put us out of business? Surely it was enough to own Be Friendly. Did you have to nap him [15–2] as well?' That was Peter's Everest in racing. Later on, when his love affair with the *Express* soured, I tried to poach him for the *Daily Mail*. Only the intervention of the *Express*'s owner, Max Aitken, caused him to turn down an offer of the job of chief racing correspondent on the *Mail*: £12,000 a year (pre-devaluation; more than double his *Express* salary; £2,500 a year fixed expenses plus £11 a day race-day allowance; first-class travel and accommodation worldwide; eleven weeks' holiday a year; a fully maintained Jaguar XJ12; freedom to do unrestricted television work; etc. Max pleaded with him to stay on the grounds of friendship, loyalty and a modest increase in salary. Peter phoned me to tell my editor, David English (now Sir David) that he had reluctantly succumbed to Max's personal plea. As Peter wrote in his autobiography *Calling the Horses*, 'I bogged it all right' – for soon after this Max was forced to sell the paper and Peter was to say goodbye to the *Express* after all.

For much of Peter O'Sullevan's time on the Express, *Valerie Frost was secretary to the racing team – which role afforded her a special perspective on the O'Sullevan personality.*

Valerie Frost

At the time I joined the *Daily Express* as racing secretary in 1960 I was equipped to work for the perfectionist that Peter O'Sullevan is because I had come straight from Newmarket and employment with the Queen's martinet of a trainer Sir Cecil Boyd-Rochfort – another for whom the best would barely suffice. Throughout my years at the *Express* Peter worked, and I mean worked, seven days a week – writing and broadcasting – because there was always copy to be produced on Sunday for Monday's paper.

In fact he would think nothing of phoning his article from Paris on Sunday after racing at Longchamp; catching a late flight out of Orly; picking up his Jag at Heathrow and strolling into Ayr racecourse, 400 miles north, on the Monday in search of a story or a bet – or both.

He hated coming into the office and would phone from draughty callboxes (in the pre-mobile days) to request the next day's betting forecasts, usually while Clive Graham was dictating his article to me. There was keen rivalry between the two but never enough to breach their underlying friendship. If Clive picked up the phone before me, he'd hand it over with a pretence of annoyance, announcing: 'His Master's Voice'!

Months would sometimes go by without his making an office appearance, and although I would cope with most of his mammoth mail myself some letters required a personal reply and these would swell in volume after a long period of absence.

On one rare appearance he was wearing a beautiful new suit just collected from his tailor, so I greeted him with the words: 'Nice whistle!' 'Yes,' he said, fingering the collar of the impeccably cut jacket, 'but look at this.' He was indicating one hand-made stitch fractionally out of alignment which an electronic microscope would have had difficulty in locating. 'It will have to go back, won't it?' And it did, of course.

During the salad days of the Be Friendly/Attivo era I always wore supporter outfits in various combinations of black and gold. On one occasion I was sporting a very smart black Louis Feraud trouser suit with a specially commissioned yellow turban and shoes. On seeing me at the racecourse, his only comment was: 'You shouldn't wear yellow shoes with black trousers'! Knowing him for an enthusiastic bird-watcher, I pointed out that snowy egrets had black legs with bright yellow feet and he surely approved of them. 'Of course,' he responded, adding 'and you bear very favourable comparison. But the snowy egret, or *Egretta luma*, never encroaches on to the racecourse.'

After each of Be Friendly's Vernons November Sprint triumphs he threw marvellous office lunch parties, taking over the cellars of Ye Old Cheshire Cheese in Fleet Street, importing a piano and pianist and placing a bottle of claret with an individually printed label before each guest. After customary meticulous planning he was unable to attend the renewal in 1967 through bronchitis and, doubtless, exhaustion. He was driving more than 1,000 miles a week at that time in restless pursuit of excellence, and I remember the forecast of one guest to the effect that 'He'll burn himself out by the time he's fifty.' It is remarkable that, thirty years later, he is still the leader.

Since the day I started working with the *Express* I have never been less than totally proud of working for him. Apart from 'the voice', the figure and the clothes, he has an elusive charisma that makes him stand out in a crowd. Arkle had it, Desert Orchid had it, Milton had it; Peter O'Sullevan has it!

Christopher Poole, racing correspondent of the London Evening Standard, *is an unashamed fan of O'Sullevan the journalist.*

Christopher Poole

As my dear old mother was wont to remark: the appearance of ease is often the result of hard labour.

Loved a cliché or two, did Mum. Peter O'Sullevan, on the other hand, has always managed to avoid them. But hard labour, in his case consisting of painstaking hours spent in research, certainly makes for apparent ease. As that magnificent, mellifluous voice clicks into overdrive, the admiring listener can be forgiven the impression that O'Sullevan's outstanding skill as a commentator is effortless, God-given in fact. Well, hardly. He has always worked at it. Lonely work; hours of it. Making sure he knows not only the colours carried by every jockey in every race but each horse's physical characteristics, quirks of nature and perceived abilities. For each moment at the microphone, a hidden agenda of background.

Peter O'Sullevan approached his work as a racing journalist in much the same way. Having learned his craft with the Press Association during an era when being on the staff of that agency was anything but a sinecure, he joined the *Daily Express* in 1950. That paper was his journalistic base for thirty-six years, for twenty-four of which he worked in harness with the late Clive Graham. Together they formed the most formidable and widely respected team in the business.

I first met Peter O'Sullevan in 1960, by which time he was looked upon with something close to reverence by his colleagues. His book of contacts throughout international racing had become all-embracing; his knowledge of the form book was exceptional; his ability to write informed, current copy on a daily basis without peer. Yet to a younger man just starting out he was unfailingly attentive, polite and helpful. He was then, and remains to this day, my hero. But he was also my object of envy. When, without fail each morning, I would read the O'Sullevan column, frequently the thought would cross my mind that I was in the wrong game. How could I ever hope to challenge his matchless grasp of racing?

The answer, of course, was that I couldn't. What is more, I never have. Like all writers on this subject who reached professional maturity during the O'Sullevan years, aiming to be second best was the pinnacle of realistic ambition. Some mornings his article would contain quite enough facts to have lasted us lesser scribes for a week. They were crammed with 'stories' about horses, their owners, trainers and jockeys, overflowing with facts and big-race running plans. What is more, we knew the copy to be accurate.

Additionally, he would tip winner after winner. In one never-to-be-forgotten spell, he napped twenty-two successful horses from twenty-four selections. One season, four of his five Classic naps triumphed. Each day, it seemed, on the racing pages of the *Express* would appear a 'boast' listing yet more O'Sullevan victories. Punters, of course, loved him. Yet he remained modest, almost shy.

Calling the horses became Peter O'Sullevan's trademark. In essence, no one has done it better. But the other string to his bow must not be overlooked. This remarkable man was also the most accomplished racing journalist of his day in the written word. Gradually, I learned that it was futile to try to emulate him. There is only one Peter O'Sullevan; so basking in the reflected glory he has brought to the specialist craft of calling and writing about the horses is the only way to go with a degree of self-respect.

If this reads like a fan letter, that's because it is. I have been an admirer for nearly forty years and see no good reason now not to stand up and be counted.

Peter O'Sullevan has done a great deal of work for the Horserace Writers'
Association, as George Ennor, President of the HWA from 1974 to 1994,
explains.

George Ennor

It was very flattering to be asked in the early 1970s if I was prepared to
follow in the footsteps of Clive Graham and take over as President of the
Horserace Writers' Association when he decided that he had filled that
role for long enough. Clive had been very much responsible for the
revamping of the old Racecourse Press Committee which, admittedly in
a climate far less friendly between press room and officialdom than it is
now, had tried to improve working conditions for racing journalists and
obtain some degree of acceptance for them. I was well aware that Clive
would be a very hard act to follow, but hoped that, with a period of
learning under his wing, I would be sufficiently versed in matters to be
able to succeed him effectively when he retired from the role.

Sadly, though, things were thrust upon me in very different circumstances. Clive never recovered from a car accident in the spring of 1974,
and died in August of that year. Suddenly, whether I liked it or not, I
had become President of the HWA – there was no question of any
election nonsense. It did not take long for me to realize that what I had
taken over was no sinecure, and I had plenty on my hands if I was to
keep up the momentum of goodwill and achievement which Clive had
generated. I did not baulk at the prospect, but I certainly thought about
it.

Peter may never have seen himself in the role of a knight in shining
armour, or certainly not as far as I was concerned, but I have not the
slightest doubt that without his guidance my early days as President
would have stumbled from one crisis to another. Peter had for many
years been Clive's comrade-in-arms, both on the *Daily Express* and with
BBC television. He knew how things worked around the hierarchy of
racing; he could advise whom I should see to discuss improvements or
alterations in any particular area. He may not have felt like an elder

statesman all those years ago, but as far as I was concerned he certainly was, and I could not have done without him. 'If I were you I would go and have a word with so and so about that; he's the fellow who can help get that sorted; have you written to him about this?' Such advice was frequently given and invariably acted upon. It did not always get the response we had hoped for, as racing's sense of PR was not far out of its infancy all those years ago; but I have no doubt that without Peter's tactical and tactful expertise the association would have achieved far less, or at best taken far longer to achieve it.

As is the case now, our flagship day was the Derby Awards lunch, which had also been Clive's brainchild. Peter's support as the association kept it going and tried to improve upon it was invaluable; he could also always be relied on to bring a large party of guests, whose enthusiasm for the venture was a big help in building its reputation.

Peter has given so many racing people so much pleasure and so many moments to enjoy over the years with his expertise behind the microphone. But there is another side to him, as many can and will testify. The support and encouragement he gave me when I took over as President of the HWA is something for which I shall be eternally grateful.

John de Moraville, son of trainer Captain John de Moraville MC, sometime colleague of Peter O'Sullevan's at the Press Association, joined the Daily Express in 1974.

John de Moraville

It was an eye-opening experience for a young and 'green' racing journalist to work in the old *Daily Express* sports department in Fleet Street. That was back in the years of the grimy but atmospheric 'old' technology, when newspaper offices had a special feel about them. Characters abounded, and although lunches lasted long into the afternoon, deadlines – hours later than nowadays – always seemed to be met!

In those days I used to answer the telephone with a fair degree of trepidation. 'May I speak to Peter O'Sullevan?', the caller would enquire. Fat chance! 'The Voice', if not commentating for the BBC, would be out in the field, reporting action from some far-flung outpost like Wincanton or Catterick. There were no mobile phones, remember, so yours truly would be taking messages, pen quivering, from some of the biggest names in the game – Turf legends that under normal circumstances I would hardly have dared address. It might have been Ryan Price, Noel Murless, Lester Piggott, Vincent O'Brien – you name him. This was the real world of racing journalism. They were the top dogs of their day – the names that really mattered. And they had a story for Peter O'Sullevan.

Peter was a journalist apart – and not only because he was a loner, and abhorred working in a pack. Price, the most controversial trainer of his time – remember the Rosyth and Hill House Schweppes sagas – was guarded at Findon by a Rottweiler of a secretary. But it went without saying that Peter, a close friend, gained uninhibited access. And Lester, who only mumbled indecipherably – and that's if you were lucky! – at most other hapless hacks, made a happy habit of divulging to O'Sullevan his innermost secrets. They included, almost annually, the exclusive revelation of what he would be riding in that year's Derby.

It was before my time, but in 1962, the year of the infamous Tattenham Hill pile-up, the perennial question of 'What will Lester ride in the Derby?' had been amended to 'Will Lester be available to ride at all?' Piggott had been summoned to Jockey Club headquarters (in those days at Cavendish Square) over his riding in a Lincoln seller of Ione, a dramatic market drifter (from 4–6 to 11–8) who had been beaten by a gambled-on stable companion Polly Macaw (3–1 to evens), and he faced a suspension that would rule him out of the premier Classic.

In that era the Jockey Club made no statements after enquiries before their findings were published in the following week's *Racing Calendar*. So the journalist's only source of information was the interviewee himself. Here was the chance of a major scoop. The ingenious O'Sullevan rang his dentist who, as luck would have it, practised across the square from the Jockey Club, and asked the nurse if there was a crowd outside number 15. He parked his grey Jaguar below the nurse's window, she gave the sign when Lester emerged into the street, and our hero shot round the corner and plucked the Long Fellow from among a posse of bewildered photographers and reporters. 'They've done me – not only for Epsom but Royal Ascot too,' reported Lester, 'and I didn't do anything wrong.' Bob Ward, trainer of both Ione and Polly Macaw, had put up the big-name jockey on the lesser-fancied horse to get better odds about the winner. What a story!

'I wasn't desperately popular with my colleagues,' O'Sullevan reflected later. But they soon forgave him. For Peter has always been regarded with enormous respect and affection by both subjects and press-room associates alike.

4

'It's a good thing for the rest of us you can't do under twelve stone'

Peter O'Sullevan and the jockeys

"And another thing, according to O'Sullevan, right now you're supposed to be leading the field by six lengths with one furlong to go."

Unusually among racing journalists – and probably uniquely among racing journalists who have not themselves experienced race-riding at the highest level – Peter O'Sullevan has always enjoyed the trust and respect of jockeys. He came close to having that vital experience: in February 1941 he was due to partner his own horse Wild Thyme in a novices' chase at Plumpton, only to be diagnosed as having pneumonia the day before the race. Frenchie Nicholson (David Nicholson's father) took over on Wild Thyme. They pulled up, and the O'Sullevan race-riding career never did get past the starting tape.

Although he never got to ride under Rules, Peter O'Sullevan did once enjoy a dream of a ride – as described in his piece 'A Hundred Monkeys' in the 1961 edition of Cope's Racegoer's Encyclopaedia, *published by the bookmaking firm run by Alfred Cope.*

Peter O'Sullevan

If it hadn't been for Alfred Cope I would have abandoned the idea on the spot. There was still time. And apprehension was rapidly getting the better part of valour.

I mean, anyone who tries to tip winners most days of the week can make a big enough fool of himself already without trying to ride one. Especially if his disability as a horseman is on a par with mine. And lack of skill apart, as if this wasn't enough, there was the no slight matter of excessive weight – represented by an undesirable frontage, fostered more by the need for consolatory than self-congratulatory refreshment.

'Poor form of amateur rider'; I could visualize my dear colleagues' headings already. I was resolved. I would withdraw. After all, what was a £25 fine compared with the alternative self-inflicted indignity?

I would diet, practise assiduously, and postpone the whole venture until better qualified. Meanwhile I was indisposed.

It was while walking to the weighing room to put resolution into effect that I met Mr Cope. Removing his horn-rimmed spectacles, as if they were no longer trustworthy, he confessed – as though apologizing to himself – that he had read my column that morning. And he had inferred, no doubt mistakenly, that I was to ride in a race here at Epsom this very afternoon.

'I am,' I said, his conciliatory tone suddenly dispelling caution, 'I am.'

Mr Cope's composed reaction was such as can only be achieved by one inured to shock by a lifetime's experience of the racing world. With masterly diplomacy – suggesting simultaneously an obligation to place the House of Cope at a disadvantage and a reluctance to part a client from his money – he said, 'You can have 100–1 if you would like a bet.'

'Monkeys,' I remember replying with hilarious abandon, 'a hundred monkeys.'

Thus committed, events developed so swiftly as to defy coherent recollection. There was the agony of apprehension in the dressing room as perspiring jockey's valet, Ernie Hales, requested, 'try holding in your breath' – I hadn't exhaled for three minutes – as he strove to fasten the top button of my breeches . . . There was Scobie Breasley's tender enquiry as to the present rates for passenger freight insurance.

I remember wishing I knew the answer to the child's query – 'what's that one going to do, Mummy?' – during my uncomfortable progress, on wafer-thin soles, over the hot tarmac between weighing room and waiting car . . . the voice of ITV paddock commentator Robin Hastings, 'they are all very calm here except Peter O'Sullevan who is sweating freely' . . . Cyril Mitchell's request for 'the other leg' before he deftly manoeuvred me into the saddle. And the shock of landing on it.

I remember Alec Marsh's gleeful 'I hope you will find no grounds for criticizing the start . . .' and the reflection that the cry 'they're off' might have singular significance. But it didn't. We started 'on terms', as they say.

After two furlongs I'd resolved to give up smoking; after half a mile to forswear drink and, approaching Tattenham Corner, to give up riding. But not for nothing was I familiar with *The Rae Johnstone Story*. I recalled how he assessed the opposition at this stage and I looked up to count five white behinds ahead. Fool I was not to have worn binoculars, instead of goggles, to bring them closer. But my gallant partner, eager to be home and shed his burden, was doing that. Each time I switched numb fingers to a new grip – if only they'd plaited the reins instead of his mane – we overtook another.

Now I knew all the sensations of being a jellyfish. One to beat and we were upsides. Such a hive of desperate activity, too (surely Sir Gordon had retired?) and I remembered how I had praised jockeys for sitting 'mouse-still' on a dying partner. Here was a unique situation. It was the rider who was dying. And victory so near. I pinched myself to affirm reality, missed and evidently tweaked my partner. For he lunged at the line, placing our unity in further peril in the process, so that when I heard the loudspeaker announcement 'photo-finish', I knew we'd won.

Considering that I had beaten most of their naps, I must say my colleagues on the press put on a very brave show. I had never experienced such an unrestrained feeling of affection for all my fellow creatures – though I must say I thought the *Daily Sketch*'s Norman Pegg could have phrased his question – 'Have you ever been on a horse before in your life?' – with more becoming tact. Geoffrey Gilbey had, he said, taken photographs of me 'in a great variety of positions'. I thought Lester Piggott was overdoing it a bit when he observed, drily, 'It's a good thing for the rest of us you can't do under twelve stone.'

And I never heard the end of Lord Rosebery's remark which began 'Well, you may not be much of a writer, but . . . ' because at that moment an imperious tap on the shoulder commanded my attention. This was surely the ultimate accolade – an invitation to the Royal Box. Probably it was the Duke himself. I looked up expectantly. But he wasn't the Duke of Edinburgh and he looked very like my sports editor, Bob Findlay. 'Wake up,' he said. 'Wake up, you've got ten minutes to turn in some copy.'

Well, I suppose that's as near as I'll get to a hundred monkeys. But, as Mr Cope reflected, 'It would have been very annoying if the Tote had paid 200–1.'

Calling the Horses *describes how in the late 1940s trainer Keith Piggott had phoned Peter O'Sullevan during the Lincoln meeting which then opened the Flat season: 'Can you look after the boy and give him a lift to Aintree?'*

'The boy', a cherub-faced teenager who had ridden his first winner in 1948 at the age of twelve, grew into one of the greatest Flat jockeys the Turf had ever seen: Lester Piggott.

Lester Piggott

I've known Peter since the beginning of my riding career, and a measure of the durability of our relationship is that he commentated on my first victory at Royal Ascot – Malka's Boy in the Wokingham Stakes in 1952 – and my last – College Chapel in the Cork and Orrery over forty years later in 1993.

Back when I started race-riding the Flat season opened at the end of March at Lincoln, and moved on to what was then a mixed Flat and National Hunt programme at the Grand National meeting at Aintree. Being too young to drive myself, I would have a lift from Lincoln to Liverpool with Peter, and these cross-country trips – no motorways in those days – formed the early basis of our friendship. As a young jockey there were occasions when I certainly needed a friend in racing, and it was always a big help to me that Peter was lending support.

You did not have to know Peter long before you realized that he was the best-informed journalist around, and the best connected. A fluent speaker of French, he came to be on such good terms with the top trainers across the Channel that his pre-season reports from the French training centres in the 1950s and 1960s became essential reading, not only for punters but also for British trainers and jockeys trying to weigh up the strength of the overseas challenge for our top races.

As a commentator Peter is the best there's ever been. The key to his quality was always preparation: not only studying the colours of every jockey, but familiarizing himself with the characteristics of each horse.

It's well known that Peter likes a bet, and maybe the personal involvement in some of the races he was calling made him that bit sharper!

I rode for him several times. When I partnered Be Friendly in the Challenge Stakes at Newmarket in October 1969 that great horse was a five-year-old coming towards the end of his career, and not the force he had once been. But I won two races on Attivo in 1978 – both at Lingfield Park. Attivo, by then aged eight, was a front-running horse who always liked to be going on, so you had to make plenty of use of him in a race. Peter was adamant that his horses should not be knocked about: 'Don't hit him more than twice' was his regular instruction, but with Attivo once was enough.

Peter has been a friend all my riding life, but more than that – he's always been on my side.

With Vincent O'Brien at Goodwood, 1990. Gerry Cranham

With Lester Piggott (still showing the signs of a recent fall) at Sandown Park, 1980. Gerry Cranham

Be Friendly (Geoff Lewis) beats So Blessed (Jimmy Lindley) in the Palace House Stakes at Newmarket, 1969.

*Attivo (Roger Wernham) pips Kambalda (Philip Waldron) in the 1974
Ladbroke Chester Cup.*

*In the weighing room at The Curragh, 1975, with two Irish champion jockeys –
Wally Swinburn (diamonds) and Johnnie Roe (sash).*

(Overleaf) The PO'S racecard for the Martell Grand National, 1996.

Handwritten top: 1996 37tv NATIONAL 3 6 8 9 11 12 15 [16] 19 22 24 25 27 28

Handwritten: 3 6 Becher C V Chair B C V

7/17/9/18/1

Handwritten left notes:

1982 Grittar last winning fav

1923 Sergeant Murphy (last (13) yr winner.

78 FIRST-TIME RIDERS (27)

This year 5 Irish-trained = Last win (1975) 21 years ago L'Escargot. (15 Irish ents Itis yr)

Four miles about four furlongs, for seven yrs old and upwards

Third Race **3.00 THE MARTELL GRAND NATIONAL STEEPLE CHASE (HANDICAP) (CLASS A)**
(Estimated total value £250000)
(Grade 3)

The breeder of the winner, if qualified under Order 196, will receive a Breeder's Prize of £5075
82 entries, 12 at £100, 22 at £350, 16 at £600 and 32 at £900.-Closed January 24th, 1996
Owners Prize Money. Winner £107427; Second £45552; Third £22652; Fourth £10386; Fifth £4921; Sixth £2942.
(Penalty Value £142534)
Weights raised 9lbs and Order 95(ii)(c) complied with where applicable

W 22

Form		Owner		Trainer	Age	st	lb	

27 Chris Maude 2nd

1 0 YOUNG HUSTLER. *3rd attempt*
1U3BP5 Ch g Import - Davett
C Mr Gavin MacEchern ....(N. A. Twiston-Davies,Cheltenham) 9 11 7
DARK BLUE, YELLOW stripe, YELLOW sleeves, DARK BLUE armlets and star on YELLOW cap. C. Maude
15/58

28 Charlie Swan 6th

"Will miss race it soft" O'B

2 0 LIFE OF A LORD. *Kerry Nat. Winner*
6-3U1P Br g Strong Gale - Ruby Girl
Mr M. J. Clancy ....(A. P. O'Brien,Ireland) 10 11 6
RED, YELLOW spots, ROYAL BLUE cap, YELLOW spots.
(Breeder - John Costelloe) 
10/43

21 Tony McCoy 2nd

3 0 DEEP BRAMBLE.
1P0-4 Ch g Deep Run - Bardicate
Mr Paul K. Barber ....(P. F. Nicholls,Shepton Mallet) 9 11 5
Mr Mick Coburn
DARK GREEN, WHITE chevron, LIGHT GREEN sleeves, DARK GREEN and WHITE check cap. A. P. McCoy
(Breeder - J. Mernagh) 
9/25

29 Conor O'Dwyer 4th

4 0 SON OF WAR. *1981 Russ. jury. (35 yr)*
-45F42 Gr g Pragmatic - Run Wardasha
Mrs Vera O'Brien ....(Peter McCreery,Ireland) 9 11 0 *1st ruver*
PINK, BLACK hoop and armlets, striped cap.
W PH Jameson
(Breeder - Michael J. Corbett) 
7/34

25 Warren Marston 2nd

5 0 LUSTY LIGHT.
PF-P43 B g Strong Gale - Pale Maid
P-F Mr B. R. H. Burrough ....(Mrs J. Pitman,Upper Lambourn) 10 10 11
LIGHT BLUE, ORANGE chevrons, LIGHT BLUE sleeves and cap.
(Breeder - Thomas Doherty) 
10/31

30 Carl Llewellyn 5th
W92

6 0 PARTY POLITICS. *W 92 2nd 95*
3P2-P B g Politico (USA) - Spin Again
Mrs David Thompson ....(N. A. Gaselee,Upper Lambourn) 12 10 11
PINK, PURPLE cross belts, hooped sleeves, PURPLE cap. C. Llewellyn
(Breeder - D. R. Stoddart) 
8/26

25 Mick Fitzgerald 2nd

7 0 ROUGH QUEST.
22F12 B g Crash Course - Our Quest
Mr A. T. A. Wates
Lady Wates ....(T. Casey,Dorking) 10 10 7
NAVY BLUE, GREEN sash, CERISE cap. M. A. Fitzgerald
(Breeder - Michael Healy) 
5/26

28 Jonathan Lower 4th

8 0 CHATAM (USA).
20P3 B g Big Spruce (USA) - Cristalina (FR)
Mr Adrian F. Nolan ....(M. C. Pipe,Wellington) 12 10 3
Dr B. Nolan
ROYAL BLUE, EMERALD GREEN epaulets and armlets.
(Breeder - Alec Head) 
9/37

32 Richard Dunwoody 11th
W86,94

9 0 SUPERIOR FINISH. (SUN Competition)
3315 Br g Oats - Emancipated
Mr G. Henfrey ....(Mrs J. Pitman,Upper Lambourn) 10 10 2
WHITE, BLACK hollow box, BLACK and WHITE halved sleeves, BLACK cap. R. Dunwoody
PETER McGRANE (Breeder - Mrs Jane Cowley) 
7/34

23 Tom Jenks 3rd

10 0 CAPTAIN DIBBLE. *Wn 92 Scottish Nat.*
70-U B g Crash Course - Sailor's Will
Mrs R. Vaughan ....(N. A. Twiston-Davies,Cheltenham) 11 9 12
RED, EMERALD GREEN star, EMERALD GREEN and RED hooped sleeves, RED cap, EMERALD GREEN star.
(Breeder - Mrs Liam O'Donnell) 
9/28

26 Trevor Horgan 2nd

11 0 RUST NEVER SLEEPS.
2-45 B g Jaazeiro (USA) - Alice Kyteler
Mr D. M. Murphy ....(Donal Hassett,Ireland) 12 9 12
DARK BLUE, ORANGE sleeves, LIGHT GREEN and MAUVE striped cap.
(Breeder - Mrs V. McCalmont) 
8/54

12 BISHOPS HALL 10 9 11
Br g Pimpernels Tune - Mariner's Dash
Mr R. Alner .... (R. H. Alner,Blandford)   Mr M. Armytage
GOLD, BLACK hoops, SCARLET cap.
(Breeder - William O'Gorman)

Mr Marcus Armytage 5th
W90
4P2 ~~Front runner~~
9/59 XJ

13 WYLDE HIDE .... *Dual Chguites winner* 9 9 8
B g Strong Gale - Joint Master
Mr J. P. McManus .... (A. L. T. Moore,Ireland)   *1st to do 50*
EMERALD GREEN and ORANGE hooped, WHITE cap.
Wtg | 3 Hurdles
(Breeder - Paul Ryan)

Frank Woods 2nd
Paddy won 2 Irish Nat'l
von Aide - Hurdles.
311
7/17   SNB

14 ANTONIN (FR) 8 9 7
Ch g Italic (FR) (pedigree untraced) - Pin'Hup (FR) (pedigree untraced)
G. R. Bailey Ltd (Baileys Horse Feeds)   J. Burke
.... (Mrs S. A. Bramall,Thirsk)
YELLOW, DARK GREEN stripe, striped sleeves, quartered cap.
(Breeder - Pierre Sayet & Maurice Marlin)

John Burke *
Youngest *
David Walsh
P603
7/39

15 RIVERSIDE BOY .... (13) 9 7
Ch g Funny Man - Tamorina
Bisgrove Partnership .... (M. C. Pipe,Wellington)
LIGHT BLUE, BROWN epaulets, sleeves and cap.
(Breeder - Miss M. Sherrington)

Rodney Farrant 3rd
So double Banger year
4P5
7/35

16 BAVARD DIEU (IRE) 8 9 5
Ch g Le Bavard (FR) - Graham Dieu
Saguaro Stables .... (N. A. Gaselee,Upper Lambourn)   J. F. Titley
YELLOW, EMERALD GREEN and YELLOW halved sleeves,
EMERALD GREEN and YELLOW quartered cap.
(Breeder - Noel McGrady)

Jason Titley 2nd
W95
6/33 *Ch/2 white hind sox white B Gaze*

17 ENCORE UN PEU (FR) 9 9 5
Ch g Nikos - Creme Caramel (FR)
Mr Vincent Nally .... (M. C. Pipe,Wellington)
EMERALD GREEN, RED Cross of Lorraine, RED sleeves,
EMERALD GREEN armlets, RED cap.
(Breeder - Ecurie Decrion)

David Bridgwater Bre
0222
5/34

18 SIR PETER LELY 9 9 2
B g Taeroso (USA) - Picture
John Doyle Construction Limited
.... (M. D. Hammond,Middleham)
YELLOW, BLACK braces, armlets and spots on cap.
(Breeder - Highclere Stud Ltd)

Mr Chris Bonner 2nd
PF
11/40

19 BRACKENFIELD 10 8 13
Ch g Le Moss - Stable Lass
T. and J. A. Curry .... (P. F. Nicholls,Shepton Mallet)   Guy Lewis
PURPLE and WHITE diamonds, WHITE sleeves, PURPLE armlets
and diamond on WHITE cap.
(Breeder - C. Kenneally)

~~*Youngest*~~ *
Guy Lewis
15/29

20 OVER THE DEEL *212 1995* 10 8 11
Ch g Over The River (FR) - Cahernane Girl
Mr George Tobin .... (J. Howard Johnson,Crook)   *Littlewoods organised comp*
LIGHT BLUE, PINK sleeves, LIGHT BLUE and PINK check cap.
DAVID DAVIES, 19, (Breeder - Conor Hynes)
Mr Tim McCarthy
604
10/52

21 INTO THE RED 12 8 8
Ch g Over The River (FR) - Legal Fortune
Mr J. Huckle .... (J. White,Aston Rowant)
Miss E. Saunders   Richard Guest
YELLOW, WHITE cap, DARK BLUE star.
(Breeder - M. W. Hickey)

Richard Guest 4th
570F
5/47

22 GREENHILL RAFFLES .... *PETER RUSSELL* 10 8 8
Ch g Scallywag - Burlington Belle
Mr D. A. Price .... (P. J. Hobbs,Minehead)
Mrs S. P. Marsh   M. Foster
ROYAL BLUE, WHITE cross belts, RED, WHITE and BLUE *(Lucinda Russell)*
quartered cap.
(Breeder - J. L. C. Shedden)

Martin Foster 3rd
40
7/27   SNB

Ch white Blaze

23 VICOMPT DE VALMONT 11 8 8
B g Beau Charmeur (FR) - Wish Again
Mr John C. Blackwell .... (P. F. Nicholls,Shepton Mallet)   P. Hide
BLACK, RED hoops, BLACK sleeves and cap.
(Breeder - Roland Rothwell)

Philip Hide 2nd
6/27 XJ

24 PLASTIC SPACEAGE *BRUISED FOOT* (13) 8 6
B g The Parson - Chestnut Fire
Spaceage Plastics Limited ...... (J. A. B. Old,Wroughton)   G. Upton
BLACK, YELLOW chevrons and armlets, hooped cap.
(Breeder - M. Hourigan)

~~*Guy Upton 3rd*~~
8/38

25 OVER THE STREAM 10 8 6
B g Over The River (FR) - Bola Stream
J. D. Gordon & E. C. Gordon ..... (K. C. Bailey,Upper Lambourn)   A. Thornton
RED, BLACK triple diamond and sleeves, RED cap, BLACK
diamonds.
(Breeder - Jack Sutton)

Andrew Thornton *
amateur Champ 92/3
34
6/28   SNB

26 THREE BROWNIES 9 8 6
B g Strong Gale - Summerville Rose
Mrs A. M. Daly .... (M. F. Morris,Ireland)
ORANGE and EMERALD GREEN diabolo, EMERALD GREEN cap,
WHITE star.
(Breeder - N. J. Connors)

Paul Carberry 2nd
3 parts BRO Last of the Brownies 4th 89
4/34

27 FAR SENIOR 10 8 6
Ch g Al Sirat (USA) - Ross Lady   *Bit isse Swiss bred*
Mr P. Wegmann .... (P. Wegmann,Gloucester)   T. Eley
RED, WHITE Cross of Lorraine and sleeves.
(Breeder - W. O'Dwyer)

Tim Eley *
11/41

28 SURE METAL .... (13) 8 6
B g Billion (USA) - Sujini
Mr L. A. Morgan .... (D. McCain,Cholmondeley)   D. McCain
ROYAL BLUE, WHITE sash and armlets, quartered cap.
(Breeder - Mrs R. A. Thomas)

Donald McCain *
4-5
8/40   XJ

SNB

Sounding off at a Jockeys' Association dinner, flanked by (left to right)
Joe Mercer, Paul Cook and Lester Piggott.

Greeted by Her Majesty Queen Elizabeth The Queen Mother at a party hosted by
Dick Wilkins (left). Thomas Jaski Ltd

Turf talk: conversations with two of the late greats of British racing – Jim Joel (above) and Sir Gordon Richards.

Sitting for sculptress Angela Conner. Paul Ross

Lester Piggott's great rival in the 1950s and early 1960s was the Australian rider Scobie Breasley, four times champion jockey in Britain, whose close friendship with Peter was highlighted by his partnering Be Friendly to victory in that colt's second Vernons November Sprint Cup in 1967. The following year the day of the Sprint Cup, 9 November, was to be the very last day of Scobie's glorious riding career in Britain. He describes one of racing's most famous anti-climaxes . . .

Scobie Breasley

I got to know Peter well soon after I settled in England in the early 1950s, and like all jockeys found him exceptionally clued up about what was going on in racing. One year I persuaded him to come out to Australia, and at the Melbourne Cup meeting at Flemington they got him to call one of the races. Then as now, the standard of commentary on Australian tracks was very high, and I like to think that the experience of visiting Australia and hearing and meeting some of our best commentators might have honed his own skills a little. Not that his skills had much room for improvement! He was by far the best commentator in England, and effortlessly retained that position for decade after decade.

Peter was very instrumental in getting me my first rides for Vincent O'Brien, a role for which I had good reason to be extremely grateful to him. At the time I did not know Vincent well, and when John McShain, owner of Gladness and Ballymoss, was looking for an English-based jockey, Peter kindly recommended me – with the result that I won the Sunninghill Park Stakes at Ascot in July 1957 on Gladness, and the following year the Coronation Cup, Eclipse Stakes, King George and Arc on Ballymoss, certainly one of the greatest horses I was ever privileged to partner.

But another of my all-time favourites had an even closer connection with Peter: Be Friendly. A lovely big chestnut with no vices at all and blessed with phenomenal speed, he was an absolutely top-class sprinter, certainly one of the best I ever rode. A measure of his class is that as a three-year-old he won the seven-furlong Two Thousand Guineas Trial at Kempton Park, even though he was not a seven-furlong performer at all: his class got him through. I won five races on Be Friendly including the King's Stand Stakes at Royal Ascot and the Vernons November Sprint Cup on the second occasion he won the race, in 1967.

The day of that same race the following year, Saturday 9 November, was the last day of the 1968 season, and my final day in the saddle, and I was confident of being able to sign off my career in the best possible manner with a big-race victory on one of my favourite horses (Be Friendly was a certainty) for one of my dearest and oldest friends. A perfect way to end!

It did not work out as it should have. I stayed overnight near the course, and first thing on the Saturday morning woke to find the area laying under a blanket of heavy fog. This was unsettling but not, on the face of it, disastrous, as the weather was reported to be fine and sunny – a beautiful day – just a few miles away, and the fog would surely lift.

When we arrived at the course I started to get worried, as the fog showed every sign of spoiling the party by refusing to go away, and the stewards had to put back the time of the first race. After a while, with still no sign of the fog's lifting, they put back the start of the programme yet again. Ever hopeful, I changed into Peter's familiar yellow and black silks and weighed out, but the fog would not take the hint. Eventually the meeting was abandoned and we all trooped disconsolately away.

That day was one hell of a kick in the backside for me, and I was desperately sad to be denied the perfect ending. But Peter took this reverse extraordinarily well. He knew we couldn't do anything about it, so he just shrugged his shoulders and put the crushing disappointment behind him.

Typical of the man.

A measure of the regard in which professional jockeys have held Peter O'Sullevan over the years is that for over a quarter of a century he has been an honorary member of the Jockeys' Association. Michael Caulfield, currently Secretary of the Association, pays his respects.

Michael Caulfield

That Peter O'Sullevan was elected an honorary life member of the Jockeys' Association in 1970 was a fitting tribute to his standing among professional riders. Most jockeys have a less than charitable view of the opinion of journalists who have never experienced race-riding at first hand, but with Peter the situation was different. His deep understanding of the sport, and the common sense which informed his strongly held opinions about concerns close to jockeys' hearts such as the use of the whip, was such that his opinions always counted. Jockeys have long known that, win or lose, in Peter they have a great ally, a man who will always be supportive, always appreciating the peculiar pressures of the jockey's lifestyle.

When in 1990 the Association instituted its annual awards dinner – now the Lesters – Peter was an immediate supporter, and since the inaugural dinner has been an invaluable presence as co-host of the evening, even when the pressures of Cheltenham or Grand National homework were providing a powerful distraction. His close links with what is now one of the great social events of the racing year, and his contribution to the sport in general over half a century, were recognized at the 1996 dinner when he became the very first recipient of an honorary Lester.

That award celebrated a multi-faceted contribution to racing over the decades – as journalist, owner, highly successful punter – but it has been particularly as a television commentator that he has carved out his unique niche in the history both of racing and of broadcasting, and to mark his award that night we replayed three of his most memorable commentaries: Red Rum and Tommy Stack winning the 1977 Grand National; Aldaniti and Bob Champion landing the National four years later; and Dawn Run and Jonjo O'Neill on that never-to-be-forgotten afternoon at Cheltenham in 1986.

Some of Peter's ringing phrases from those famous occasions – 'A tremendous reception – you've never heard one like it at Liverpool!' . . . 'Here comes John Thorne, fifty-four-year-old John Thorne putting in a storming finish' . . . 'The mare's beginning to get up!' – will sit in the folk memory of British sport alongside Kenneth Wolstenholme's 'They think it's all over – it is now!' at the end of the 1966 World Cup Final.

It was that commentating voice which first drew me, like so many others, into racing. In my case it was the 1968 Grand National: at the age of eight I heard Peter calling home Red Alligator and Brian Fletcher, and was hooked. Later the same year I heard Kenneth Wolstenholme describing the majestic performance of Bobby Charlton when Manchester United beat Benfica to win the European Cup at Wembley, and I was hooked on soccer as well!

With his extraordinary feel for all aspects of racing, Peter is a part of the heritage of the Turf. He has long been – and will long remain – a true hero of the jockeys.

The one person guaranteed not to be hearing a Peter O'Sullevan commentary at the climax of a famous race is the winning jockey, though plenty of top jockeys will admit to digging out the video of their greatest triumphs and reliving them with 'The Voice'.

Tommy Stack, whose victory on Red Rum in the 1977 Grand National was the occasion of perhaps the most memorable O'Sullevan commentary of all, holds him in the highest esteem.

Tommy Stack

One remarkable aspect of Peter, so far as a jockey is concerned, is his knack of relating to what the rider is doing in a race: he understands why a jockey is making a particular manoeuvre. His other great characteristic, invaluable for a trainer or a jockey, has been his discretion and integrity. If you tell Peter something which you don't want to get around, there's no danger that he'll make use of it – he'll just lock it away and take it no further.

His knowledge of racing for so long has been unbelievable, and for years he had better insight into the French scene than anybody else. Indeed, he brought an air of authority to everything he did.

I don't think we'll ever see his equal, and I'm only glad to have been a jockey in his era.

As stable jockey to Jimmy FitzGerald at Malton, Mark Dwyer has ridden in the O'Sullevan colours.

Mark Dwyer

I schooled Peter's good horse Amigos over fences at Jimmy FitzGerald's and we were all very excited about him as a potential novice chaser. When I rode him in his first novice chase, at Musselburgh in January 1996, he ran and jumped brilliantly, and halfway up the final straight, with two fences to go, he was absolutely skating up. Then after two out I felt him go: he'd broken down badly, and there was no option but to retire him from the fray for the time being and let him have plenty of time to recover.

This was a great blow as Amigos had showed such promise, but Peter as usual was very philosophical about it: if the horse needs time, he'll be given time.

From the jockey's point of view, Peter is an ideal owner. He won't burden you with elaborate instructions other than to look after the horse. He loves to have a punt and that can add a little edge, but he always has the interests of the horse at heart.

I've always thought he had a bit more interest in the jumpers than he did with the Flat, and he certainly has a very profound knowledge of the sport – not many owners are as well informed as he is. And as for his commentaries – the simplest way to put it is that it was Peter's commentary which made the great races great. If you watch again and again one of those great Cheltenham occasions – as I occasionally do, rewatching my Gold Cup victories on Forgive'N Forget or Jodami – you know the result, but watching is still exciting, thanks to the magic of Peter's commentaries.

5

The overseas connections

Born in Ireland, raised in England and from his early career a close follower and interpreter of the racing scene in France, Peter O'Sullevan has long had an international view of racing.

The esteem in which he is held in his native Ireland is attested by the message from Mary Robinson, President of Ireland, at the front of this book, and by the bestowal in 1993 of the Par Excellence Award from the Racing Club of Ireland in recognition of his services to the sport. His affinity with the racing scene in France has been a feature of his journalism since its early days. But his influence has stretched much further than Europe: he has commentated in Australia, South Africa and many other countries – and in October 1980 called, to an invited audience in London, the Turf Classic at Aqueduct, New York, the first race transmitted live via satellite.

Kevin Smith, chairman of the Racing Club of Ireland, expresses the affection of the Irish.

Kevin G. A. Smith

Born near Ken*mare* (you could bet there would be a horse there from the beginning), Co. Kerry: supreme horse-racing commentator, top race selector, successful owner, campaigner for animal rights, humorist, philosopher and gentleman. There is enormous affection and respect for Peter in this country. For me, 'exemplary professional' are the words that always come to mind in thinking about Peter – which puts him in the same premier league as Vincent O'Brien and Lester Piggott. Moreover, whenever I have had the opportunity to speak to Peter, in person or on the telephone, I find a great feeling of warmth coming through.

At the Racing Club of Ireland Annual Awards Dinner last year, President Mary Robinson recalled that Peter O'Sullevan, 'the unmistakable voice of racing', was often heard in the family home as she was growing up. At our 1993 dinner, Peter received the Club's Par Excellence Award (one of only six to receive this award to date, the others being Vincent O'Brien, Lester Piggott, Pat Taaffe, Martin Molony and Michael O'Hehir) for 'his outstanding contribution to the enjoyment of racegoers and the benefit of punters over the years'. I was then reminded that in drawing together a collection of writings on Irish agriculture and the British market – for a pamphlet published by TUAIRIM (Irish for 'opinion') – in 1965 I had observed that we were indeed fortunate to benefit from the favourable image generated for Ireland by a number of unpaid 'ambassadors', one of whom was Peter O'Sullevan.

On the morning after the 1993 dinner, Peter and I attended at the Racing Apprentice Centre of Education in Kildare to witness the then Minister of Agriculture perform a ceremony to mark the construction of new facilities there. We were due to be at Turf Club Headquarters within the hour, where a luncheon was being hosted for members of the Racing Club of Ireland. By the time the Minister arrived we were already under pressure to leave and, as he went on a bit, I whispered to Peter, 'If he doesn't finish in five minutes, I'm going.' Peter exclaimed, 'You can't do that!' and then quickly added, 'Bet you a tenner he finishes in five.' We got to the Turf Club (almost on time) with the tenner in Peter's pocket – I was still the student and he the master. Mind you, I also took his advice about Lemon Souffle in the Moyglare that day and, using her as a banker, collected a share of the jackpot!

Also at that dinner, Peter gave a marvellous exhibition in auctioning a copy of *That's Racing* – which he and Sean Magee edited to benefit the International League for the Protection of Horses – to raise funds for the Irish Society for the Prevention of Cruelty to Animals. Former President of the Circuit Court and Turf Club, Steward Judge Frank Roe, remarked: 'I wish he was selling my horses.'

Another Irish racing man with a special regard for Peter O'Sullevan is the indefatigable Finbarr Slattery, Manager of Killarney racecourse from 1978 to 1991.

Finbarr Slattery

Back in my student days when I was following the horses more than was good for me, Peter O'Sullevan's broadcasting career as a racing commentator began. Right from the start he had a captivating voice that made you sit up and take notice.

Early on in Peter's era, after a colleague of his in the broadcasting world had called the wrong result in a big race, 'Larry Lynx' (the racing correspondent of *The People*) was on his sick bed listening to a race being broadcast in which he had a special interest. The horse he had tipped in his paper to win the race duly obliged. Larry told the readers of *The People* his reaction: 'When I heard the melodious voice of Peter O'Sullevan stating that my horse was winning, I knew it was my horse and no other horse.' Larry Lynx was having a dig at the commentator who called the wrong result!

When I was appointed Secretary/Manager of Killarney Races I was very hopeful that I'd get Peter O'Sullevan to attend the races there. I wrote inviting him, but he was unable to come. Killarney races would have been Peter's local meeting had racing been alive and active there in his youth, for he was born in Kenmare, twenty miles from Killarney, in 1918. Unfortunately, there was no racing in Killarney from 1903 to 1935, so Peter missed out.

I was at the helm in Killarney for the fiftieth anniversary of the revived meeting in 1986. To mark this great occasion I invited many racing scribes to contribute to a book which I brought out to mark the golden jubilee of continuous racing on Killarney's present track. Peter O'Sullevan was one of those invited and he turned up trumps with a beautiful gem recalling Stanerra's great win in the Japan Cup.

I had retired from the racecourse by the time of the tribute day for Michael O'Hehir, but was responsible for this special event. Among those invited to come along and pay their tributes to Ireland's most famous radio and television commentator was Peter O'Sullevan. Peter duly arrived the previous evening and it was while I was awaiting his arrival that it dawned on me to entitle my forthcoming book *Following the Horses*. I mentioned this to Peter on his arrival at the Great Southern Hotel and he seemed very pleased with the idea. Famous people from all over Ireland attended Michael O'Hehir Day at Killarney races, but I have no doubt about the person whose attendance gave most satisfaction to Michael – none other, of course, than Peter O'Sullevan; and Michael acknowledged this fact in his book, *My Life and Times*, which was published shortly before he died on 24 November 1996.

I wrote to Peter regarding the address he gave on Michael O'Hehir Day: 'You had tears flowing from men who wouldn't cry in a hundred years!'

Peter O'Sullevan's departure from the commentator's chair will leave a void that will be very hard to fill. No matter how good his successor is, Peter was special to the airwaves and it was great to have lived through it all and enjoyed his melodious voice for so long.

One of the great characters of Irish racing is trainer Mick O'Toole, a long-time friend of Peter O'Sullevan's.

Mick O'Toole

I feel like I've known Peter for ever!

I started to get to know him well once I was going racing in England regularly. For Ascot meetings I used to stay with Jack Doyle at The Foresters, near the racecourse, where Peter would always stay, so I could see at first hand his dedication and meticulousness. Every morning he'd have breakfast on his own – and likewise he'd be alone at dinner in the evening – so that he could concentrate on his homework.

We were always fascinated by his dedication, but wouldn't dare intrude on him, he was so wrapped up in what he was doing. Peter was one of the most committed journalists around, and would go out to the track for the early morning sessions with the great Ascot trainers of that era, Vincent O'Brien and Paddy Prendergast. We'd stand in the background and try to eavesdrop, catching the words of wisdom passing between him and those great trainers.

In 1975 there were eight Irish-trained winners at Royal Ascot – seven trained by Vincent and the eighth, Faliraki in the Norfolk Stakes, my own first winner at the Royal Meeting. Peter joined us that evening for a great night out! He'd been out on the track that morning to see Lester work my horse, and having found out how impressed Lester was with Faliraki had a nice touch on him.

Peter has always been a fellow who could beat the odds for you, and over the years had the occasional bet for me in England: he backed Dickens Hill each way before that horse was runner-up to Troy in the 1979 Derby, and we had a good touch when Dickens Hill went on to win the Eclipse Stakes the following month.

When the BBC was covering the Cheltenham Festival, Peter would interview me for television during the early morning sessions out on the course. But I could never find out where he stayed for the Cheltenham meeting: he used to secrete himself in a hideaway so that he wouldn't be distracted from his homework.

In 1996 it was a great honour and a pleasure for me to be invited to a dinner in London for the Queen Mother, hosted by Bob McCreery and Peter. The other guests included trainers Roger Charlton and Jimmy FitzGerald, the Queen Mother's racing manager Michael Oswald and the Roux brothers, and it was a wonderful occasion – worthy not only of the Queen Mother but of Peter.

He may be not far off eighty, but he doesn't behave like an old man. After the 1996 Irish Derby at The Curragh, I asked Peter if he could give the Newmarket trainer Neville Callaghan a lift back to Dublin Airport. Neville rang me the following morning and said: 'Peter may be nearly eighty, but he drove back to Dublin like a fellow of twenty! We got there in half an hour, the fastest ever!'

In June 1977 Peter O'Sullevan's Daily Express *column from Royal Ascot carried the story of 'a slim, soft-spoken 26-year-old Southern Irishman whose wagers are still the talk of an incredulous betting ring'. This punter – whose Royal Ascot bets that year included losing £32,500 on the Coronation Stakes and £39,000 in the King Edward VII Stakes before ending the meeting 'about 2,000 quid in front' – was soon to become one of the legends of the betting scene, and of Irish racing: J. P. McManus.*

J. P. McManus

The greatest compliment I can pay Peter is that he's the only racing journalist who could ring my home, and my mother would talk to him! She always took great pleasure from Peter phoning: she never felt he was in a hurry. But any other journalist – racing or otherwise – got the deaf ear.

My memories of Peter the commentator go back to the days of Arkle. When that great horse took on Mill House in their first Gold Cup in 1964, the build-up to the race was intense. It was run on a Saturday that year, and as not every house had a television in those days many of the neighbours came in to watch the race on our set – and to listen to those unmistakable Peter O'Sullevan tones describing one of the greatest races of all. Parts of that commentary remain lodged in the memory: 'This is the best we've seen for a very long time!'

From an early age I was very interested in betting, and soon came to learn the tell-tale signals in an O'Sullevan commentary. When he said of your horse, 'He has it all to do,' you could tear up your ticket there and then!

He is not only a marvellous commentator, but a great man to read a race as well as calling the horses. It's easy enough for me if I'm watching a race in which I've had a bet: I just have to concentrate on one horse. Peter has the ability to be aware of so many different things at the same time – a real gift. He mixes the ability to see the complete picture – breeding, betting, race-reading – with extraordinary attention to detail: you'll see him going round, making sure he knows the Christian name of each jockey in a race, or checking the correct pronunciation of the horses' names.

I first met Peter at Ascot in 1977, but long before that had idolized him as a commentator and admired him as a journalist: he never wrote anything that wasn't a fact, and I always respect anything Peter has to say. As we got to know each other we'd share information. In 1983 I had a horse named Bit Of A Skite, which we thought could be something very special for Cheltenham. About a month before the big meeting he ran an absolute blinder when an outsider in the Arkle Perpetual Challenge Cup over two miles at Leopardstown. His trainer Edward O'Grady, a great man to train a horse for the big occasion, decided to aim Bit Of A Skite for the four-mile National Hunt Chase for amateur riders at the Festival meeting. Three weeks before Cheltenham we took Bit Of A Skite back to Leopardstown for a racecourse gallop: Jonjo O'Neill schooled him, just to teach him to pop round, and on getting off after the school asked whether we were sure we were putting him in the right race, as this horse was good enough to go for the Sun Alliance Chase. Since by then the Cheltenham bookmakers were not going to be over-generous to me when I was backing my own horses, I decided to keep the National Hunt Chase, the easier option, as the target.

At this time Bit Of A Skite contracted a poisoned foot, and the black-smith had to dig deeper into his hoof than he would have liked to remove the infection. As a result the hoof had to be filled with Polyfilla! In addition to his poisoned foot, the horse was also afflicted by very bad joints. Between then and Cheltenham the horse never saw grass and the only way Edward could keep him fit was by swimming. We finally got the horse to the races in one piece, which in itself was no small feat. But after initially telling Peter how special this horse was and the great things we expected from him, I felt I had no option but to advise him not to back him because of all his problems. Imagine how I felt when I met Peter in the unsaddling enclosure after the horse won: I didn't know whether to laugh or cry. But we got back what we'd lost at Cheltenham – or rather, what felt like losses – when Bit Of A Skite went on to win the Irish Grand National at Fairyhouse.

Peter loves to have a bet, and I find him an excellent man to run something by before we go into action. He's always been a team player:

no matter what he knows, he never uses it against you, and would never try to get a fancy price for himself before you'd got on.

Everything Peter does, he does remarkably well, and brings the absolute best out of everybody – jockeys, trainers, waiters, whatever. He recently conducted a charity auction for me in Ireland, and I have no doubt that were it not for his presence that evening, we would not have made anything like the amount we did – he simply demands the attention of the bidders for items which they otherwise might ignore. It was lucky for racing that he chose the sport as his professional field, as he must rank as the sport's greatest ambassador.

A magic man.

One famous Irish racehorse whose exploits are intertwined in the memory with Peter O'Sullevan commentaries was of course Arkle, the peerless chaser who between 1962 and 1966 won twenty-two of his twenty-six steeplechases, including the Cheltenham Gold Cup three times. The jockey who rode Arkle to all his chasing victories, Pat Taaffe, died in 1992, but his son Tom, now a trainer in Ireland, has fond memories not only of the great horse but of the man who so often called him home.

Tom Taaffe

I sat on Arkle when I was two years old – so I can safely claim that Arkle was the best horse I ever rode! – and naturally associate so many of my father's great victories on him with Peter. Their wins in the three Gold Cups and the two Hennessys are inseparable from Peter's commentaries, and watching recordings of my father and Arkle is simply not the same if Peter is not commentating. In fact it sometimes seems as if all my good racing memories are accompanied by the O'Sullevan voice.

I first met Peter when, some time in the mid-1970s, I was taken up to the commentary position at Aintree: Michael O'Hehir was up there with him, and to be in the presence of the two commentators who'd meant so much to me was wonderful. Peter was very welcoming, but I particularly recall his asking whether I had a cold: if I was going to start coughing I'd better stay well clear!

Another great Irish chaser whose biggest victories were called by Peter O'Sullevan was L'Escargot, who won the Cheltenham Gold Cup in 1970 and 1971 then turned his attention to the Grand National: third behind Red Rum and Crisp in 1973 and runner-up to Red Rum the following year, in 1975 he became the only horse apart from Golden Miller to win the Grand National and Gold Cup. L'Escargot was trained by Dan Moore, whose son Arthur now trains from the same yard.

Arthur Moore

So many of my earliest racing memories have that unique Peter O'Sullevan commentary as accompaniment, and more recently it has been a privilege to get to know Peter well. It was a particular honour to be invited in May 1996 to one of the lunches in London which, with Bob McCreery, Peter co-hosts for the Queen Mother – a truly memorable occasion.

When Royal Bond ran in the Cheltenham Gold Cup in March 1981 we wanted to have an ante-post interest, so the previous November I asked Peter to back him for me. He got on at 66–1 and we promptly sent him our cheque – at which he announced that it was very unlucky to send payment for an ante-post bet before the race had been run! Doubtless Peter was right, as Royal Bond started in the race at 10–1 but was pulled up.

During all those years that the BBC covered the Cheltenham National Hunt Festival, the encounter with Peter during the early morning sessions out on the track formed a highlight of the week – especially when an Irishman named Des Ellison was in attendance, giving the assembled company – and Peter himself – the benefit of his Peter O'Sullevan impressions!

If Ireland is literally Peter O'Sullevan's homeland, France has been very close to his heart since he first visited the country in the early 1940s. His pre-season reports from the leading French stables became essential reading for the English racing community at a time when French-trained horses were mounting regular challenges for the English Classics, and his close connections with France have continued to the present day. Louis Romanet is Secretary General of France Galop, the French equivalent of the Jockey Club.

Louis Romanet

Peter O'Sullevan has always been considered in Great Britain as 'the voice of racing'. One of the characteristics of the coverage of racing on television in Great Britain is the quality of the commentators, and Peter O'Sullevan has certainly been the outstanding one. I have been personally impressed by the fact that you could close your eyes to hear his commentary and see the race as real, such was the quality of the description. The tone of his voice was itself a part of his reputation, recognized as it was by everybody.

One of the very special aspects of his career is that, visiting France occasionally as an English commentator for the Prix de l'Arc de Triomphe or other big races, he received the same recognition in our country. Peter always had a great affection for French racing, dating back to the 1940s. Before the Longchamp stands were rebuilt in 1966, he had to commentate on the Arc from the top of the roof of the grandstand, and as he says, 'My concentration was split between describing the race and making sure my feet didn't slip off two planks.' He was very disappointed when we left the Eurovision, and so the BBC, to sign a contract with Channel Four in 1986 for the coverage of French racing on English television. When the contract was given to the BBC again in 1995, I had an immediate call from Peter telling me how delighted he was to be back to commentate on the Arc and other big French races.

He will certainly remain the best racing television commentator of the century, and after his retirement, we will continue to hear his voice with great pleasure in past recordings. The racing world needs popular people to promote its activity, and Peter has certainly been a major contributor.

I must say that I will always regret that he never became a French racing commentator.

French trainer François Doumen caused a considerable stir in British jump racing when sending over Nupsala to beat Desert Orchid at 25–1 in the King George VI Chase at Kempton Park in 1987. Since then he has become a familiar presence on the National Hunt scene, especially through the exploits of The Fellow, winner of the Cheltenham Gold Cup in 1994 after being beaten a short head in the race in 1991 and 1992 and finishing fourth in 1993.

François Doumen

In December 1990 I brought The Fellow, owned by the Marquesa de Moratalla, across to Kempton Park for the King George VI Chase, and the Marquesa introduced me to her great friend Peter O'Sullevan. What struck me straight away about Peter was his calm, his *phlegme britannique*. I was very new to English racing and it was rare for a French trainer to send horses over, but Peter was to prove a catalyst between me and the English scene, and ever since has proved an invaluable ally: we have enjoyed some fruity coups together!

The Fellow, only a five-year-old, finished third behind Desert Orchid in that King George, and then his target became the 1991 Cheltenham Gold Cup – in which he just failed, by the width of a Gauloise, to reach Garrison Savannah. The following year he was again beaten a short head in the Gold Cup, this time by Cool Ground, and in 1993 ran fourth behind Jodami. When he finally got what he deserved so richly and won the race in 1994, I swear I could detect a shift in the O'Sullevan tones at the climax of his commentary – the usual velvet transformed to corduroy.

Peter has been an always dependable reference point for my contact with English racing, and I've felt very flattered and honoured that a man of his calibre should go out of his way to give me his support. With his unceasing sense of perspective on the racing world, and good-humoured understanding of the people in it, he's been as stable as a rock.

One of the most significant French connections which Peter O'Sullevan has enjoyed has been with Alec Head, trainer of 1956 Derby winner Lavandin.

Alec Head

I first got to know Peter when I started racing in England: I rode Le Paillon to be second in the Champion Hurdle in 1947. (That horse went on to win the Prix de l'Arc de Triomphe: it wouldn't happen nowadays that a Champion Hurdle runner-up would win the Arc!) From then on I raced in England a good deal, and Peter and I became very friendly – he was without doubt my best contact across the Channel. I had the highest regard for him as a journalist, and it was through his *Express* articles, as well as our regular personal contact, that I was able to keep abreast of what was happening on the English racing scene.

When I started training, Peter used to come and take a tour of the horses in France to find out about our Guineas and Derby horses who hadn't been seen out in England. After his visit to our stable in the spring of 1956 he alerted his readers to the chances of our Derby hope, Lavandin, and Peter's support for the horse was instrumental in his being backed down to favourite. When Lavandin won the Derby by a neck under Rae Johnstone, it was a wonderful moment.

Peter is a man of great heart, and has always been a perfectionist in everything he does. Not long ago I saw him at the Cartier Awards dinner in London, when I received an award for my 1996 July Cup winner Anabaa, and was struck by what wonderful shape Peter was in, mentally and physically.

So why on earth is he planning to retire?!

6

The missing letter 'e'

Peter O'Sullevan and charity

11ᵗ October.

Dear Peter,

Just to say a very big thank you for conducting such a successful Auction for us last Tuesday. Nobody else would have extracted such figures. We were thrilled and overwhelmed at the generousity of those present.

I gather you got hold round to George Welham before I did! I must try and look in at their exhibition next week.

Thank you Peter, from us both.

Yours ever.

Valda.

___

The updated edition of Peter O'Sullevan's Calling the Horses, *published in 1994, closes with the author's vote of thanks to various animal charities he has supported – 'And to all whose aim is to add the missing letter "e" to the human race.'*

Ian Carnaby's article in the Sporting Life *following Peter O'Sullevan's Hall of Fame award from Help The Aged in November 1995 paid due recognition to a vital aspect of the O'Sullevan persona.*

Ian Carnaby

For a man with effortless grace, Peter O'Sullevan's view of personal appearances is disarmingly downbeat. 'I detest speaking in public and dislike having a camera pointed at me,' he said. 'But one thing I seem to have an aptitude for is auctioneering. I enjoy it because you have something specific to do. You coax a response from the audience, and an empathy develops.' At the last count, that empathy was worth not far short of £2.5 million. That is the sum raised by O'Sullevan for more than thirty charitable causes since he started out well over forty years ago. This marvellous achievement was honoured at the London Hilton yesterday, when the Princess of Wales presented racing's most famous broadcaster with the 1995 Hall of Fame award, judged by Help The Aged. The Princess is patron of that organization.

It is no great surprise that O'Sullevan manages to accept the onset of 'old age' with his characteristic wry smile. Apart from anything else, he happens to be the quickest-witted 77-year-old around; this much became perfectly clear when I spent a few hours with him.

A list of the charities to have benefited from his friendly persuasion includes most of the famous names. Everything from the British Red Cross to the Greater London Fund for the Blind is there, with a massive £305,000 (what an auction that must have been) raised for Irish Hospices along the way. There was also the appeal on behalf of Stoke Mandeville, and the treasured letter of thanks from Jimmy Savile which followed. For twenty-five years, O'Sullevan has run the auction on the eve of Timeform's Charity Day, and there have been almost as many similar occasions on behalf of the Stable Lads' Welfare Trust. Add to that his unstinting efforts on behalf of the two projects he holds most dear – the Brooke Hospital for Animals and the International League for the Protection of Horses – and it may safely be assumed that time spent outside the commentary box has not been exactly frittered away.

He has never accepted a fee for auctioneering, but realized about ten years ago that there was another way of supporting the Brooke and the ILPH. He simply asked for 5 per cent of the money raised to be divided between the two organizations, a scheme invariably approved by whichever committee was making the decision. 'I also struck up an effective partnership with Charles Benson,' he explained. 'I was the sort of straight man, if you like, but Charlie really got the audience going. He just insulted people in that rather special way of his, but they loved it and no one ever took offence. When it came to getting them to dig deep into their pockets, we were a very good team.'

In the particular area of animal charities, O'Sullevan is uniquely well placed to comment on individual successes. He is happy to dwell on these, but only if people acknowledge the huge amount of work still to be done.

'In the late sixties, I had an idea for Royal Ascot,' he recalled. 'I was looking through the jockey bookings, and wondering who would ride most winners. I rang Gerald Green at Ladbrokes, and suggested running a book on it. "I'll have to think about it," he said. "Well, don't think too long," I replied. "You've got about an hour!" Apart from anything else, I wanted the story as an exclusive in my *Daily Express* column. Anyway, various London clubs were interested in the sponsorship angle, and we ended up with the Ritz Club Trophy. Princess Anne, as she then was, became involved and the cheque to the winning jockey was divided between the Injured Jockeys' Fund and a named charity, in this instance Riding for the Disabled. After a while, I asked for one half to go to the IJF, with the other half split between the Brooke Hospital and the International League. And don't forget, I was commentating on the races, so it was easy enough to slip in a few words about the charities on television. A surprising number of people rang up wanting to know more.'

There are examples of quite extraordinary generosity. In 1983, the Horserace Writers' Association organized an auction which raised £36,000 for the Brooke and the ILPH. The Queen Mother presented a carriage clock, and Sheikh Mohammed contributed a nomination to Jalmood.

The memory brings on a warm glow, but anyone who has read O'Sullevan's autobiography, *Calling the Horses*, is well aware there is still a mountain to be climbed. Mercifully, the most grotesque excesses, with horses in some countries worked literally until they drop, and others shipped in the most appalling conditions to some bleak abattoir, have been curbed. O'Sullevan's commentary on a documentary about the Brooke Hospital, which was established by Dorothy Brooke in Cairo in 1934 and now has nine 'offshoots' in Egypt, Jordan, India and Pakistan, stresses what may be achieved through straightforward education. The message is simple enough. 'We must alleviate ignorance, and persuade. If you look after your animals, you will get better service out of them.'

More recently, and much closer to home, the television programme *They Shoot Horses, Don't They?* distressed many viewers. But whatever methods it employed in other areas, at least it drew attention to the splendid work done by Carrie Humble, who runs Britain's only registered charity for former racehorses – the Thoroughbred Rehabilitation Centre at Kendal. O'Sullevan gave her maximum encouragement, while warning that the going would be far from easy.

'Rehabilitation of horses is so important,' he said, 'but Carrie has had to do everything off her own bat, even using her own money. She should have been able to pay her assistants a proper salary, but received hardly any support. I really do think various bodies could look at their own role in all of this. For a start, the Racehorse Owners' Association seems not to involve itself in welfare, but leaves everything to the individual's conscience. The ROA could show a sense of responsibility and make a small donation now and again.'

O'Sullevan wonders if an only child has more affinity with animals. Anyone watching him at the age of seven might have guessed that his life would be given over to them. 'My grandmother was a very good horsewoman, and when people came to stay they often brought their hunters with them,' he recalled. 'But one day I felt deeply affronted when my pony was turned out of his box to accommodate one of them. It was pouring with rain, and I'm afraid I went missing. After a while, my grandfather, the deputy Lord Lieutenant of Surrey, became concerned and alerted the police. Some time later, they reported that a small boy had been spotted in the fields on the Reigate road, holding an umbrella over a pony. Many years afterwards, a journalist was kind enough to remark that I'd been holding up a metaphorical umbrella ever since! But if you really want to know why I'm involved with animal charities, it's because I think we should be *responsible*. If we're the superior beings, we're responsible for the lesser ones.'

No one listening to this quiet, modest, supremely dignified man will be in any doubt that, in his case, the responsibility has been discharged quite magnificently.

Ian Carnaby's article drew attention to the Thoroughbred Rehabilitation Centre in Cumbria. The star turn of the TRC is the 1984 Grand National winner Hallo Dandy, who fell on hard times after his retirement but is now the flagship of Carrie Humble's campaign for a more responsible approach to the post-racing lives of racehorses.

Carrie Humble

In 1988, on my return to England after living in the USA for seventeen years, I began to get involved with Thoroughbred horses – initially by buying an old gelding named Folklore. I stabled Folklore with a friend's father who bred racehorses, and started helping the stable get horses fit prior to going to the sales. The sales themselves proved to be a real eye-opener. I was amazed at what sort of horses you could buy for £500 – and equally amazed at who was buying them! This set me thinking about the dreadful wastage of good young horses who were going through public auctions, and I realized why retired racehorses have acquired such a terrible reputation when put to other uses. No one seemed to be giving them the chance to be properly 'converted' – hence the alarming instances of decline and neglect.

It was then that the idea for the Thoroughbred Rehabilitation Centre – a place dedicated to retraining ex-racehorses – took hold, and shortly afterwards I was given the best piece of advice I ever had: 'You should talk to Peter O'Sullevan.'

Having been out of the country for so long I could scarcely remember who the man was, but tracked him down and, with my passion for my crusade conquering shyness, simply phoned him up and asked him how I should get started. His response to this call out of the blue from what must have sounded like a somewhat cranky lady was typically down-to-earth and practical: You must become registered as a charity, he told me, and then I can give you practical help.

Once the TRC had been registered, that help came immediately and unstintingly. Peter supplied me with the names of others in the racing business who could help, and – most important – his own avowed support for the Centre lent a credibility which otherwise I would have spent fifty years slaving for. His name opened doors, and the respect in which he is held throughout the racing world has proved an invaluable asset – quite apart from the substantial sums of money he has personally donated to the TRC over the years.

Peter is one of the very few people in racing prepared to put their head above the parapet for *the horse*, which after all is the single most important player in the game and yet is too often forgotten once racecourse glory has passed or (more commonly) has never come. To have someone of his calibre lending me very public support when I was a completely unknown quantity has been like a gift from God. No amount of money could have bought the sort of influence which his reputation and standing were able to exert.

Since those early days of the Thoroughbred Rehabilitation Centre I've been privileged to sit with Peter on committees addressing issues of equine welfare, and have come to an even greater appreciation of his depth of concern for the horse.

The TRC would not exist today without Peter's support. He has truly been my knight in shining armour – and such a gentleman that on a more personal note I have to confess that were he thirty years younger and not happily married to Pat, he'd be in some trouble from this quarter!

The International League for the Protection of Horses is a well-established charity devoted to the welfare of horses throughout the world. Peter O'Sullevan has long been a fervent supporter of its aims, and in 1992 co-edited the book That's Racing, *all proceeds from which went to the ILPH.*

George Stephen

I doubt if any individual has done more for the International League for the Protection of Horses (ILPH) than Peter O'Sullevan. He has been an active member for so long that nobody can remember when he first joined. He does not go out shaking tins or partake in flag-flapping demonstrations. He just quietly takes a keen interest in everything we do and is always ready with sage advice and the offer of help, through his multitude of contacts throughout the horse world. He turns up at awkward times, and in all weathers, to various ILPH functions, whether it be to petition government or to give his invaluable advice to the working group investigating the welfare of ex-racehorses. He never raises his voice but everyone listens when he speaks.

Peter will probably never talk to me again for saying this, but he must also be the leading individual fund-raiser for the ILPH. Again, always low-key. Every month or so, the familiar voice on the telephone would say, 'Peter here.' After a few pleasantries, he would casually mention, 'by the way, I did a lecture for such and such an organization last week and I asked them to send the cheque to the ILPH. Would you mind awfully sending them a receipt when you get it?' I have lost count over the years how often this has happened.

But Peter's greatest fund-raising contribution must be the book *That's Racing.* I am not sure how he and Sean Magee thought of the idea, but one day in late 1991 the familiar voice on the telephone outlined to me their plan to bring out a book of short, previously unpublished pieces by most of the top names in racing, on the theme of 'special racing memories'.

The response from the racing world was prompt and positive. The book was published in time to be launched at Cheltenham 1992 and is a tribute not only to the respect for Peter and Sean shown by racing people, but also to the respect they have for the welfare of the horse. No contribution had been published before; all were written at no fee; all profits from the book went to the ILPH. When everything was ready, we still had not hit on a suitable title. Peter and I met for lunch at his favourite Italian restaurant near his London home to seek inspiration. It must have been a good lunch, because suddenly we had it. 'That's racing' were the famous words spoken by the Queen Mother to Dick Francis after the dramatic collapse of her horse Devon Loch, fifty yards from victory in the 1956 Grand National. Dick thought he was for the Tower. Instead, Her Majesty said, 'Well, Mr Francis, that's racing.' It seemed a perfect title.

We left the restaurant well pleased. I got into a taxi and said goodbye to Peter through the window. As we drove off, the cabbie turned to me and said, 'That was Peter O'Sullevan, guv.' I said, 'That was quick of you, you must have seen him in your wing mirror.' 'Naw,' was the reply, 'I never saw him, but I'd know that voice anywhere.'

Another charity keenly supported by Peter O'Sullevan is Compassion in World Farming, whose Political and Legal Director Peter Stevenson acknowledges his contribution.

Peter Stevenson

Peter O'Sullevan has for many years been an enthusiastic supporter of Compassion in World Farming (CIWF), particularly in our campaign against the export of live farm animals. I first met him when we spoke together at a press conference in 1990 to launch a CIWF mass lobby of Parliament, when hundreds of people gathered from all over the country to urge their MPs to ban live exports. Peter spoke with great caring about the cruelty inflicted on animals by this trade. What struck me about Peter then – and has done so on many occasions since – is his warmth and gentleness. I remember his amusement when I confessed that one of my main pleasures in meeting him was that he knew Dick Francis, of whose thrillers I am a most avid fan.

The export of horses, donkeys and ponies for slaughter abroad has for many years been prohibited. In 1990, however, the European Community tried to force Britain to lift its ban. Peter was in the forefront of those who, outraged at the prospect of horses once again being sent overseas for slaughter, campaigned successfully for Britain to be allowed to retain the ban.

What makes Peter so unusual, however, is that – unlike many in the horse world – his concern is not limited to equines but extends to all farm animals. Time and again Peter has supported CIWF's campaigns to stop lambs and sheep being sent on horrifically long journeys to continental abattoirs and against the export of tiny calves for rearing in veal crates in the Netherlands and France. Peter has highlighted the suffering of these animals on such long journeys, stressing that they are just as worthy of our concern as horses.

I remember Peter being aghast when he first learned that the Treaty of Rome – the cornerstone of European law – classifies live animals as goods or agricultural products along with sacks of potatoes and cans of beans. He immediately joined our campaign for animals to be given a new status in the Treaty as 'sentient beings'. Such a new status would recognize that animals are not goods or products but living creatures capable of feeling pain and fear.

My most recent meeting with Peter was typical in demonstrating his modest, unassuming manner. In the summer of 1996 CIWF had organized a demonstration outside the Dutch Embassy in London to protest against the fact that many British sheep were being exported to the Netherlands and then re-exported to Greece, sometimes on journeys of over fifty hours without food, water or rest. Just as the demonstration started I noticed Peter at the back of the crowd. Without seeking any publicity for himself he had taken the trouble to join us at what for him was a very busy time of the year. He explained that his wife had told him of all the things he needed to do on his rare day off but that he had insisted on first attending our demonstration. Yet again he showed his firm determination to help end the cruelty so often inflicted in the course of the live export trade.

Richard Searight of the Brooke Hospital for Animals, founded to alleviate the suffering of animals in Cairo and now working in several other countries, offers his own appreciation.

Richard Searight

Peter O'Sullevan became a Brooke Hospital patron in 1985. He has attended several of the Brooke Hospital tea parties, held annually at the House of Commons, where he has met many of the charity's supporters. He read the lesson at the memorial service held at St James's Church, Piccadilly, in 1991 for Dr Murad Raghib MBE, who had worked for the Brooke for fifty years since joining the Hospital in Cairo in the 1940s. Peter also initiated most generous donations to the Brooke through the Ritz Club Trophy and has mentioned the Brooke Hospital at many race meetings.

He read the commentary for our films, *Your Horse and Your Family*, *Expanding Oasis* and *Sixty Years of the Brooke Hospital* about the founding and present-day work of the charity. Peter has a wonderful understanding of horses, and understands too how they can suffer. This always comes over in his film commentaries – and is why we always come back to him. We are so grateful to him for giving us this invaluable service without charge.

David Sieff, Chairman of the Trustees of Racing Welfare and Stable Lads' Welfare Trust, which looks after the concerns of the needy within the racing industry, acclaims the way in which Peter O'Sullevan has given his support.

David Sieff

Peter is not a great committee man, but he's always been concerned about people and is very charitably minded, and has performed great service for the stable lads and girls – so often the forgotten people of racing – as Vice-President of the Stable Lads' Welfare Trust.

It's just not Peter's style to stand up in the front waving his arms about and making a great noise, but in his quiet way he gets a huge amount done – and through his skills as an auctioneer: he's raised hundreds of thousands of pounds at charity auctions over the years.

The great thing about his work for racing welfare is that if he says he'll do something, then he will. You just consider it done.

WILLIAM WOOD

Turf Accountants

Telephones:	84A CHARING CROSS ROAD	MAJOR W. W. WOOD
TEMple BAR 7075	**CAMBRIDGE CIRCUS**	MAJOR A. G. SWAN
7076	LONDON, W.C.2	
7077		
7078	*Represented on the Members' Rail at Ascot and the Principal Southern Meetings.*	

P. J. O'Sullevan Esq.   19 April 1952

DATE	WIN	PLACE	HORSE OR GREYHOUND	YOU WIN £ s. d.			YOU LOSE £ s. d.		
14/4			Full Brother	6	5	–	5	–	–
16/4			Kings Prize				25	–	–
			Trinidad	5	12	6	5	–	–
18 Apr			Early Rise				4	.	.
19 April			Kings Mistake				9	.	.
			Clonmaggery	56	5	.			
			Neron	40		.			
				108	2	6	48	.	.
				48	.	.			
				£ 60	2	6			

Dear Peter,

After three years during which you have won consistently, we shall have to give you best, and ask you to bet elsewhere. You are too good for us!!

This will not, of course, make any difference to our friendship, I trust.

Yours ever,

Bill.

WITH COMPLIMENTS

7

'Owned by Peter O'Sullevan . . .'

"They've a pretty strong picket line—the Queen, the Queen Mother, Lord Derby, Peter O'Sullevan, to name but a few"

Peter O'Sullevan first owned a racehorse during World War Two, in the shape of a gelding – a half brother to the 1938 Cheltenham Gold Cup winner Morse Code – given to him by his uncle. Having billeted his acquisition at a livery stables in Richmond Park, he discovered that the horse was not the half brother to Morse Code at all, but his uncle's old hunter Hawthorn. Registered under the name Wild Thyme II, Peter O'Sullevan's first racehorse made his debut at Cheltenham in November 1940: he was pulled up.

Between then and 1966 the O'Sullevan colours of black, yellow cross-belts and cap were carried by a series of mostly undistinguished performers, with sporadic victories tending to come in selling races. The picture was transformed with the acquisition in October 1965 of the yearling Be Friendly, bought with his partner Stephen Raphael for 2,800 guineas at the Newmarket Sales. By the time he retired from the racecourse in 1969, Be Friendly had proved himself one of the very best sprinters of the modern era, his ten victories in Britain including the Vernons November Sprint Cup twice, the King's Stand Stakes, the Ayr Gold Cup and the Palace House Stakes, while in France he won the Prix de l'Abbaye and dead-heated for the Prix du Gros-Chêne.

Peter O'Sullevan's other famous horse was Attivo, winner of five races on the Flat (including the 1974 Chester Cup and Northumberland Plate) and five over hurdles (most famously the 1974 Daily Express Triumph Hurdle).

In a piece entitled 'A Popular Misconception', published in the Daily Express *in 1951 – long before the appearance of* Be Friendly *and* Attivo *– Peter O'Sullevan gave a crisp view of the nature of racehorse ownership (and, in so doing, introduced the soon to be familiar O'Sullevan character Bert at the garage).*

Peter O'Sullevan

Probably the most widespread misconception entertained in racing is that the owner has a 'touch' each time his horse wins. The most normal sequence of events is as follows.

H, being the horse, is well galloped at home. O, the owner, immediately informs all friends, including Bert at the garage, that H is a phenomenon.

T, the trainer, suggests that H (being super-H in embryo) be not fully exerted first time out. 'Of course, he'll win if he can, but it would not do him any good to have a hard race.'

O, being very wise (like all Os before they become desperate) agrees wholeheartedly, impressing trainer by adding that he abhors use of whip.

H, having been allowed to perform more or less at his leisure, runs very respectable race.

J, the jockey (fee five guineas for a ride, seven guineas for a winner) informs proud O that he 'could easily have been nearer – would be delighted to ride next time'.

O impresses friends – including Bert at the garage – by repeating J's remarks. Whispers name of course and date selected for next effort.

On 'the day', T expresses confidence – with cagey proviso that H 'will be even better next time, but is sure to be in first three'.

H finishes fourth. J explains that course did not suit H, who 'kept changing his legs' (not, unfortunately, with another H). O forgives lapse, explains reason for defeat to disgruntled friends, also to Bert, who is received without enthusiasm in 'local'.

H is launched on course which all (excluding H) consider ideal, and O's remaining friends are tipped off. H finishes third, but, as there are only seven runners, each-way bets lose. (Bert looks forward to day when petrol rationing will be reinstituted, and hopes that O will try to get extra gallon out of him.)

J says altered going did not suit H, but stranger in Turkish baths tells O that J is crooked. H did not have chance from the start.

Friendless O changes J (also garage) and places extra large bets hoping to reimburse former friends with winnings. H runs worst race yet, and J says H is running over wrong distance.

Disgusted O changes T, and new T says no wonder H runs badly. Poor H is full of w . . ms.

H, who is not full of w . . ms, but who is bored to death with New . . r-ket (as any self-respecting H would be), runs again.

T says H is very well, but disgusted and impoverished O says that is not good enough. O will not bet again until H is certainty.

Unsupported save by J. Citizen, who has nasty suspicious mind and considers H has been 'cheating' for months, and untipped save by correspondent who mistook H for H of same name who died twenty years ago, H wins at 100–6. O sells car.

The day on which fog thwarted Be Friendly's attempt to win a third Vernons and provide Scobie Breasley with a triumphant farewell to race-riding has been described elsewhere in this book. Peter O'Sullevan's long-time BBC colleague Julian Wilson has his own memories of Be Friendly's owner that aggravating day.

Julian Wilson

Is it really thirty-one years since I first voiced: 'Over to Peter O'Sullevan'? Did we really call twenty-four Grand Nationals together from the runaway romp of Highland Wedding in 1969 through to the popular topical win of Party Politics in 1992? In between there were Crisp, Red Rum and Aldaniti; and so many other famous and unforgettable days. It was always a tough ordeal for the horses, but never tougher for Peter and me than in 1970 when the commentary team was reduced from four to two. Peter and I covered the entire thirty fences. I don't know how Peter felt, but it scared the life out of me!

We travelled together to Longchamp, Chantilly, St Cloud and, memorably, Cagnes-sur-Mer. There are different versions of that expedition. What we agree upon is that it was cold, wet and windy – and that Peter came home with a raging bout of flu! We fought battles together, and occasionally against one another. Despite a common objective, we have not always agreed the identical path. But Peter's occasional conflicts with editorial elements within the BBC were always governed by the relentless pursuit of excellence.

Peter has always remained a private man, whose itinerant lifestyle and dedicated professionalism have made it difficult for him to cultivate a wide circle of friends. But his close friends are invariably friends for life. He is always an entertaining and amusing companion, with the journalist's love of good conversation – not to mention good cognac! For several years, like Peter, I lived in Chelsea, and during that time we shared some companionable evenings. My first wife, Carolyn, had many interests in common with Pat O'Sullevan: fine clothes; fabrics from Designers' Guild – and small dogs.

One such occasion was Saturday, 9 November 1968. It should have been an evening from hell. Instead it was a memorable delight.

It was the day of Be Friendly's attempt to win a third successive running of the Vernons Sprint Cup. Peter had called home the bonny chestnut in the first two runnings of the innovative all-aged sprint. Now the owner–commentator was poised to describe an extraordinary hat-trick of wins for the champion sprinter among two-, three- and four-year-olds. The going was perfect, and a month earlier Be Friendly had raised his game to peak level in beating So Blessed in the Prix de l'Abbaye de Longchamp. Scobie Breasley was booked to ride on what was to be his last day as a jockey. Peter had taken £1,000 to £100 months earlier that Be Friendly would complete the hat-trick.

It looked a formality . . . apart from one factor. In this early period the Vernons was run on the last day of the season. I cannot exactly recall the moment that the fog arrived, but by midday it had lodged in a thick, heavy pall over Haydock Park. During the next three and a half hours I was employed not as a racing commentator but as a weather analyst. Report after report went out live on *Grandstand*: 'The first race has been put back . . .' 'No obvious improvement . . .' 'The first race will now be run at three o'clock . . .' The north-west industrial shroud moved not an iota. Meanwhile, a few miles away, down the East Lancashire Road, there were clear skies and perfect visibility.

At four o'clock it was all over. Racing abandoned. Already the 4.12 train from Warrington was out of reach, and Peter very kindly offered me a lift back to London. In the desperate and confused search for a suitable epithet to describe such an indescribable day, I slammed the door of Peter's Jaguar so hard as to shatter his 'emergency' wine glass. There were only 200 miles to go . . .

On Peter's return to Chelsea, a telephone call from Be Friendly's regular jockey, Geoff Lewis, who was in Calcutta, enquired:

'How far did he win, Pete?'

The reply was carefully chosen.

To Peter's eternal credit, he, Pat, myself and Carolyn enjoyed a delightful dinner at the nearby Au Bon Acceuil. No bitterness, no retribution.

It was equally predictable that when Be Friendly was retired to stud, within weeks a valuable nomination was offered for auction, for the benefit of a racing charity.

So what *was* said on the journey from Haydock? Around Northampton I exclaimed: 'Better to have owned Be Friendly and been thwarted, than never to have owned Be Friendly at all . . .' Response: 'Amen to that.' Then I went back to sleep.

Both be Friendly and Attivo were trained at Epsom by Cyril Mitchell, who on his retirement in 1974 reflected on Peter O'Sullevan the owner.

Cyril Mitchell

I have trained for Peter O'Sullevan for almost twenty years. Having a journalist for an owner could pose all sorts of problems, but Peter never demanded anything but the opportunity to come along to my stables and talk about his horses and their future.

Planning a horse's engagements with Peter was a joy. He was interested in everything that affected their future and because of his very great knowledge of the business we both benefited from the experience. Peter was a member of the Mitchell family and his friendship extended to every member of our team.

Be Friendly was one of Peter's greatest horses – and appropriately named, as he really sums up our happy relationship. Peter has made so much of my training life a pleasure.

For the last decade Peter O'Sullevan's horses have been trained in Malton by Jimmy FitzGerald.

Jimmy FitzGerald

I've trained for Peter for years, and he's an exemplary owner as well as a great friend. He always puts the interests of the horse first, never wants them rushed, always gives them time if they need it. He also did me a great service by introducing me to the Marquesa de Moratalla, for whom I've trained many good horses.

Peter is known to enjoy a punt, and we've had some nice little days out over the years – such as when Trainglot won the Cesarewitch, or Sapience the Ebor. We've always shared information with each other. At Epsom in June 1977, I was going down to the paddock to saddle a runner in the race before Dunfermline won the Oaks for the Queen, and passing by one of the marquees was hailed by Peter, asking me to join him for a glass of champagne. I explained that I couldn't, as I had a horse in the next – but added that she might well win, and that Fair Kitty, who was running at Catterick that same afternoon, should win as well. Both did as I expected, and from the champagne he bought later that afternoon I knew that Peter had taken my advice! It works both ways: Peter insisted I back The Fellow in the Gold Cup – the year he won it, not the years he got beaten.

Some years ago I was at the Stable Lads' Boxing evening in London, where Sir Gordon Richards was guest of honour. At one end of the dining room was a large screen, on which they showed a film of Sir Gordon winning the 1953 Derby on Pinza – black and white pictures, no sound. Peter stood up and, quite impromptu, did a commentary on the race. He never made one mistake – it was so good it made the hair stand up on the back of your neck. And when he'd finished, the whole place erupted into applause for minutes. It was quite unbelievable – and I don't know anybody else who could have done that.

As an owner he's been wonderful. As a commentator he'll be irreplaceable.

8

'He knows how to live'

Peter O'Sullevan and the Good Life

Mr. PETER O'SULLEVAN

Peter O'Sullevan has long been known as a man not given to shunning quality in his lifestyle – at least as far as food, drink and art are concerned. In the words of Jimmy FitzGerald, 'he knows how to live'; for Albert Roux, he is 'a man of taste, a man of distinction'; and according to Peter Walwyn, 'he enjoys life to the full'.

Insistence on quality is a facet he shares with writer and famed bon viveur *Clement Freud, who focused on the O'Sullevan predilection for good food and drink in a profile in the* Radio Times *during the run-up to the 1994 Grand National.*

Clement Freud

On Friday evening Peter O'Sullevan will phone room service at his Liverpool hotel and order some poached salmon – 'They will invariably leave me a bottle of claret, which is very gracious.' Later, he will go out somewhere for a drink, not meet anyone, retire to bed early and, at 6 a.m., it is off to Aintree to see the horses exercise. There will be some horses he does not know, some of the Irish ones, and he looks at them carefully, makes mental notes: 'A couple of white feet – I'll know *you* again – wherever.'

O'Sullevan will have started 'working' on the Grand National on his holiday in the West Country in March, when there were more than fifty runners. He has pasted up the vital information on each: horse's name and age and breeding, jockey's colours, details of owner and trainer and previous form. As they jump their way around the most famous National Hunt track in the world, he calls the horses, quickly, accurately, noting who is going well, who is in the lead, in the middle section, tailed off, fallen. He thinks this is his forty-sixth National – depends on whether you count last year's fiasco, when the starter and the recall man achieved one of the great equine Horlicks of all time. As you get older, he says, you need extra insurance, have to do more homework, and are less able to cope with distractions. After his first National – fifty-seven runners, basic binoculars, winner, second and third at huge odds (Caughoo won at 100–1) – he came home and said, 'Never again.' He adds: 'Now I am just up-tight.'

O'Sullevan was born in County Kerry in 1918. His father had been a colonel, who 'seemed to be associated with a variety of regiments, was Resident Magistrate in Killarney, a charming man'. Mother, from whom the colonel was separated when their only child was very young, was English.

What do you remember? 'I am never sure what I remember and what I have been told, but I associated more with the animals of the house than the people.' At the age of six, he was deposited with his maternal grandparents in the home counties. Sir John Henry was a senior civil servant at the Board of Trade; granny canvassed for Lloyd George. The most important 'person' in his life was a pony called Fairy – on whom he rode around Tattenham Corner at the age of seven: reward for dressing up as a Red Indian in a parade at Reigate.

Were you close to your grandparents? 'I would be dealing lightly with the truth if I did not say no. I was very friendly with my pony and a goat – that's all.' His mother married again and the young Peter spent a fortnight a year with his father – 'I thought he was marvellous.' But O'Sullevan's best friends were Sir John's Russian chef and Pattenden, the chauffeur – 'I never knew his Christian name.' The principal car was a Minerva with outside gate gear change – 'At nine I could drive as well as I do now.' (He drives very well now: he once got me from Manchester to London in about an hour and a half.) I asked whether his friend the chef cooked him dishes that remained in the memory. 'I was like the poodle I now have: I preferred a cuddle to a biscuit. Had I been a horse, I would have been considered a shy feeder.'

As becomes boys of his class, he was shuttled from private to preparatory to public school. There was Hawtreys, then in Westgate: 'I am reading *Life in the Freezer* and I cannot believe Westgate was not colder. I got into Charterhouse because my headmaster had promised I'd be in the first eleven in football and cricket.' Charterhouse provided baked beans on toast and unappealing cabbage, but parents could supplement their sons' diets with special food – or send them 7s 6d a week for extra eggs and meat. O'Sullevan took the money, which went in postal orders to Glaswegian bookmakers, then the only folk licensed to transact off-course bets. In his last year at school he had 'study status' – was allowed a Primus stove, made beurre blanc without having access to a great deal of white wine and poured this over crayfish caught in the river Wey. When he left Charterhouse an uncle generously gave him 7s 6d to buy an Old Carthusian tie. He had 3s 9d each way on 'something that regrettably failed to make the first three' and had to forgo the neckwear.

At the age of sixteen, he was sent to Switzerland; he had serious asthma and developed a bad skin complaint, was more isolated than before – and away from racing, which he loved. It is, he says, very hard to eat badly in Switzerland, for they present things so handsomely. But until war began and he went into the Chelsea Rescue Service, he was in and out of hospitals and permanently on diets that were thought to be the cure for asthma and disorders of the skin: diets of buttermilk and nuts; diets of apples – nothing but apples; a diet of vegetable juices in which the main attraction was the forbidden sediment at the bottom of the glass. 'Diets introduce one to the joys of food, give one erotic dreams about roast chicken. The idea of cake, toast and tea after a long time on a diet is the ultimate luxury, quite hypnotic.'

During the war, he had a small four-seater car in which he evacuated people. He also rescued folk from bomb sites and fires and gained personal confidence. His asthma, as well as his dermatitis, improved. At the end of the war, he had a bedsit in Chelsea, his colours registered at Weatherbys and a horse in training at £4 a week – on an income of £3 14s 6d. 'Punting had to be selective and profitable. If I had a good day, it was half a bottle of Chablis and some Whitstable oysters.'

As soon as foreign travel was reintroduced after the war, O'Sullevan became a frequent visitor to France: loved driving, loved food and drink, spoke fluent French and speaks knowledgeably, fondly, nostalgically about Mère Brazier and her artichoke hearts presented with truffles and goose liver. He recalls going to the great chef Fernand Point's gastronomic temple La Pyramide at Vienne in the forties with his elegant wife Pat. It was towards the end of the Press Association reporter's summer holiday and the budget had to be carefully controlled. He'd planned the lunch to accommodate his diminishing resources, and when a dish of *foie gras en brioche* was presented with aperitifs he politely declined, before realizing that this was a delectable *amuse gueule* – a free offering to stimulate the palate. 'The surprised waiter had barely turned when I realized my error – too late. It was like calling the wrong horse – a nightmare!'

I had asked Peter O'Sullevan to lunch; he is on a diet similar to mine – no butter or rice or bread, no potatoes, carrots, pasta or spirits, no snacking between meals . . . We had agreed on black olives and quails' eggs, grilled halibut with morels, breasts of pheasant and then goat's cheese. I asked whether he would take a glass of champagne. 'Before the meal, yes. After that, red Bordeaux . . . even with fish.' He arrived dressed in a blue suit, blue shirt and bluish tie on which donkeys danced a rumba, and he brought a parcel – 'A little wine,' he said, giving it to me.

I opened the parcel. It was more than a little wine; it was two bottles and it was in no way 'little', but a first-growth claret so precious that I shall leave it in the wine cupboard to impress people. I will think long and hard about what sort of occasion it will grace: perhaps when one of Peter's horses wins an important race . . . and I organize his celebration dinner.

Albert Roux has known Peter O'Sullevan for thirty years, since the days when Roux was chef to trainer Peter Cazalet – among whose patrons was the Queen Mother – at Fairlawne.

Albert Roux

For me any race, any bumper or seller, when narrated by Peter O'Sullevan becomes a Derby. Just as Samson's strength was in his hair, so Peter's is in his voice – so beautiful, so correct. Every time he talks, I'm gripped.

He is a man of taste, a man of distinction, and one of the joys of his retiring is that from now on, when I invite him to lunch or dinner, he's more likely to be free to come!

Were I planning a menu to mark his retirement, I could do no better than the one reproduced opposite, which was prepared by myself and my brother Michel on the occasion of a dinner hosted by Peter for the Queen Mother and her favourite racing people in the cellars of Hedges & Butler in October 1985. Everybody was in fantastic form that evening – including the 'Queen Mum'.

All I would add to the menu opposite is that I would provide the great man on arrival with a glass of Krug 1985 to clear his palate, and with his coffee offer him 21-year-old malt whisky (though he might prefer a Calvados) and a little cigar – perhaps a Montecristo no. 1.

Soufflé Suissesse
served with
Reisling Les Piret 1981, Estated Bottled from Meyer et Fils

***

Ravioli de Homard Truffé Tiède, Sauce Vierge
served with
Corton Charlemagne 1982, Bonneau du Martray

****

Selle d'Agneau en Croûte au Sel
served with
Mouton Rothschild 1959

*****

Sablé au Poire sur son Coulis au Fruits Rouges
served with
Yquem 1976

****

Café et Petits Fours

***

Michael Oswald, manager of the Royal Studs, recalls an occasion when the famed O'Sullevan discernment was rewarded.

Michael Oswald

In 1978 I was with Peter on a plane going to Hong Kong for the opening of Sha Tin racecourse. Tucked away deep in Economy Class, we were not expecting anything very grand in the way of fine wines, but after we had stopped *en route* to refuel, we were served a concoction that I could only conclude had been bottled by Ho Chi Minh himself. It was quite the worst wine I'd ever tasted.

But Peter, being Peter, and his reputation and charm affecting all with whom he comes into contact, struck up a friendship with a steward who recognized him (at least from his voice) and who disappeared into First Class, emerging a short while later with two bottles of British Airways' finest claret – which turned out to be very fine indeed. These he slipped conspiratorially to us, and the rest of the flight passed off much more pleasantly than would otherwise have been the case.

It was not the first time – nor the last – that I saw the O'Sullevan influence at work!

Trainer John Dunlop, a long-time admirer and friend of Peter O'Sullevan, saw the inclination for the good life in an even further-flung part of the world.

John Dunlop

We were in Tokyo in 1983 for the second running of the Japan Cup – the first time either of us had been to Japan. After we'd been there a couple of days I asked him how he was enjoying the visit. Fine, he said, 'except I can't find a decent French restaurant'. I pointed out to him that he was, after all, in Tokyo, where they do have rather individual food – not exactly the greatest place for *haute cuisine*, at least in a French way.

But I undertook to help him in his quest, and duly discovered that there was a Tokyo outpost of Maxim's – a typically plush establishment at which I booked a table for what turned out to be a party of about a dozen, including Willie Carson, who was riding our filly High Hawk in the Japan Cup. But for Peter's insistence, I'd never have discovered that Tokyo could provide such cuisine – nor might I have discovered Marc de Bourgogne, a brandy for which he expressed a particular fondness and which one hopes did not have too great an effect on the outcome of the next day's big race.

Yet his predilection for good food and drink was never – ever – allowed to compromise the professionalism which I have so admired in him over the years. For about ten consecutive years I would ask him to come and have dinner with us one night during the Goodwood July Meeting, and always the response was the same: 'Sorry, but I'm working' – and I knew that he'd be spending every evening preparing for the following day's commentary. That was quite typical of his approach to his work.

Another outlet for the finely tuned O'Sullevan aesthetic sense is art. Claude Berry, of the Tryon Gallery in London, has seen his artistic taste at first hand.

Claude Berry

A side of Peter O'Sullevan known to few other than his friends is his love of art. He has, over the years, put together an interesting and eclectic collection of pictures and bronzes. Unsurprisingly, the horse figures prominently in his collection, but Peter's is by no means a one-track mind where art is concerned. The most unexpected theme among his pictures is the frequent appearance of clowns. As he says, 'I love the pathos and the bathos of the clown'. The international aspect of Peter's outlook is exemplified by the fact that he has paintings of clowns by French, Swiss, Flemish and Greek artists; almost the biggest canvas in his collection is that of a pierrot by the Frenchman Alain Rousseau.

No slavish follower of fashion, Peter has never been afraid to back his own judgement and he has bought several theatrical and colourful scenes of North African horsemen by the Moroccan Hassan El Glaoui. A large and dramatic picture of Appaloosas by the Spaniard Ricardo Arenys is also among the owner's favourites. Many of his pictures have been presents from friends or from his wife Pat. Into this category come seascapes by Paul Gunn, son of the famous portrait painter James Gunn, and pictures by two of the leading contemporary racing painters, David Trundley and Jay Kirkman.

Peter's friendships with equestrian artists have resulted in several of the latter presenting him with examples of their work. The outstanding Irish painter Peter Curling has made such a gift, as has the popular Johnny Jonas; another Irishman, Peter Deighan, painted Peter himself and presented him with the finished product. A less traditional portrait is that by the distinctive John Bratby. Peter particularly cherishes some etchings given to him by his wartime friend Edward Seago, and a head of his horse Amigos, presented by the artist Neil Cawthorne, brings back happy memories. Another great friend was the extrovert painter and sculptor John Skeaping, a keen racing man, member of the Royal

Academy and inspirational teacher of young artists. Skeaping's death in 1980 left a gap in many lives, but his memory lives on through his work. In addition to several Skeaping pictures, Peter has two of his bronzes, *Turned Loose* and *A Greyhound*. Skeaping is also the creator of what is, to me, the most interesting item in the O'Sullevan collection, a clay model of a pair of parakeets in the style of Henry Moore or Barbara Hepworth (Skeaping's first wife). This piece was fired by Skeaping during his year-long sojourn with the Indians in Mexico and, against the odds, survived the journey back to England. Two other bronzes of which Peter is fond are a study of Steve Cauthen by the American-based Marcel Jovine (a gift from his great friend the Marquesa de Moratalla) and a head of Desert Orchid by Simon Erland (a gift from the sculptor).

When committee members of the Society of Equestrian Artists were casting about for someone to open the first of their annual exhibitions in 1979 they decided unanimously on Peter O'Sullevan. This, to my mind, was an eloquent tribute to a knowledgeable, popular, respected and, above all, well-rounded man. A more tangible tribute is the bronze head of Peter by Angela Conner (herself a breeder of Morgan horses) unveiled at Aintree on Grand National day 1997, a gift to the course from the Duke of Devonshire. As Peter says with self-deprecating humour: 'I hope it won't frighten the horses.'

The Duke of Devonshire's choice of internationally renowned sculptress Angela Conner to undertake the bronze for Aintree is a mark of his regard for the sitter.

The Duke of Devonshire

Peter is a very old friend of mine – our friendship goes back at least as far as his fondness for my mare Park Top – and I felt that for a great many people he is not just the Voice of Racing, but in particular the Voice of Aintree. So I wrote to Lord Daresbury at the course and said that as a mark of my admiration for him I'd like to present Aintree with a bronze of Peter's head by Angela Conner, who had undertaken several commissions for me in the past. Aintree wrote back that they loved the idea, and the bronze will form a permanent tribute to a man whose contribution to the Grand National in the modern era has been enormous.

For sculptress Angela Conner herself – whose commissions have included Churchill, de Gaulle, Macmillan and the Prince of Wales – the relationship between artist and sitter is crucial.

Angela Conner

There's a threesome involved – myself, the sitter and the object. As soon as I meet my subjects for the first time, I rapidly get a feel for them, and with Peter the chemistry was right from that first moment. He's a wonderful sitter – very still and very complete – and gave me the strong feeling that he is a *good* man.

We originally planned a life-size head, then learned that Aintree intended to locate the bronze outside, so started again and worked to a larger size.

To make a portrait bust, I begin with a simple mound of clay – a neck on which is supported a 'blob' which will become the head – and then, after having made an overall assessment of the shape and nature of the particular head, start working on the details. A painting is one view of its subject; a sculpture is 365 views, as it is in the round, so you constantly have to keep the relationships between different parts of the head accurate. You cannot complete one bit and then move on to the next: at each sitting you go round and round and round your subject, building with the clay and examining the head from all angles. It is vital to keep catching unaccustomed angles, always looking for those unexpected relationships between parts of the head which make each shape unique.

I never take measurements, but rely on my eye and build up the head in an impressionistic way until suddenly along comes that moment: it's finished!

Then a new set of worries comes in. I slightly harden the clay by not watering it, then transport it ever so carefully to the foundry – which in the case of Peter's bronze is the Meridian Foundry in the East End of London. (It is a fact little trumpeted that England has the best foundries in the world.) The foundry makes a mould of the clay bust, and from that a wax version of the original is made. This is checked by the artist, signed, and

161

the edition numbered. A new 'case' is then made to cover the wax. Into this mould the liquid hot bronze is poured. The process from delivery of the clay bust at the foundry to the finished bronze takes about six weeks. After the bronze has been made, I go to the foundry and choose the particular patina required for the finish, and once that has been applied the bronze is ready for putting into position.

Sculpting a bronze is a mixture of craft – getting the shape right – and art – the spiritual activity of expressing the character of your sitter through the finished object. And the essence of the art is your relationship with your sitter.

In Peter's case it was very simple: I like him!

9

Coming to the last

14 OAKWOOD ROAD,
BRACKNELL,
BERKSHIRE, RG12 2SP

Dear Mr. O'Sullevan or may I call you Peter,!

I feel I have known you for years and felt I had to write to you and let you know that racing will never be the same once you retire.

I started watching and listening to you from a very early age (8) when my Dad would have the TV on Saturday afternoons to see racing and he had three winners at Ascot! Of course I thought this wonderful and so every Saturday I sat there glued in front of box and of course was soon "hooked". I am now 44 and feel I have known you for years!

Your presentation of horse and rider with so perfect detail and interesting facts all go a long way to say how you must spend hours sifting through information for us, the general public. I am always interested in where the horse came from, its blood lines, etc and you really do do your homework on this aspect. Not many others bother to do this, which I think is their great downfall.

— 2 —

You are and always will be "Number One" for racing, because there is and never will be a commentator like you. You are the "first voice" on racing to me and always will be.

You will be greatly missed but I do hope you will have a very, very happy retirement.

All the very best for the future.

Josephine Wanstall (MRS).

When in November 1996 Peter O'Sullevan let it be known – diffidently, almost inadvertently – that the 1997 Grand National (his fiftieth) would be his final call of that race, and that he would be hanging up the microphone for good after the Hennessy Cognac Gold Cup at Newbury the following November, the world of racing was quick to react.

The big names offered their tributes. The ordinary racegoers and television viewers sent in their letters. A man who, it had long been recognized, truly had the ability to walk with kings nor lose the common touch, was bombarded with expressions of appreciation.

Letters came from some familiar names, such as one of the great characters from an earlier age of racing coverage on 'the other side'.

John Rickman

. . . I thought I'd drop you a line to say well done with your career. Well out in front of us all and a high-class stayer too. You really have done brilliantly, Peter. Great ability, but just as important: hard and thorough work. I don't think many viewers and readers realize the hours of preparation we put into the business. Your contribution to our profession has been immense and unexcelled in the TV sphere . . .

'The rather staid headmaster of a local secondary school' in Enniskillen was moved to put pen to paper.

Bryan Gallagher

I heard that you had decided to retire and I felt that I had to write to thank you for the many hours of pleasure you have given me and millions of others over the years. I could not ever be described as a racing man and am the rather staid headmaster of a local secondary school, but I do love horses and enjoy the odd minor flutter. In common with so many others, your voice, your word pictures bring everything to life for me. It is clear to me that your preparation is utterly meticulous, your knowledge profound and when your voice goes up a couple of semitones in pitch approaching the last one or two furlongs it sends prickles of excitement up my spine! I have heard you bring all the great ones past the winning post – Arkle, Nijinsky, Gladness, Ballymoss, to name just a few – and I feel enriched by the experience. But above all, you come across to all of us as a kind, caring person, a gentle man and a gentleman.

I saw you on RTE on the occasion of Michael O'Hehir's death and you looked so well I said to myself: 'That man has the secret of eternal youth.' Whatever your secret, bottle it and sell it!!

So Peter, 'ad multos annos'. Thank you for everything. May you have a long and happy retirement.

*The Marquesa de Moratalla, owner of such familiar performers as The Fellow,
Sybillin and Trainglot, is a long-time friend and partner of Peter O'Sullevan.*

The Marquesa Soledad de Moratalla

My late brother Fon – Alfonso, the Marquis de Portago – was champion
amateur rider in France and rode regularly in England, and in 1952 I went
over with him when he rode Icy Calm in the Grand National at Liverpool –
which is where I first met Peter. He, Pat and I became very close friends –
for me they are family – and I soon discovered that he knows more about
racing than anyone.

It was Peter's profound knowledge of the sport which in 1967 prompted
my mother to ask him to find 'a really good horse, something out of the
ordinary,' for her to give me as a present. Peter suggested a two-year-old
colt coming up for auction at the Lionel Holliday dispersal sale – a colt
named Vaguely Noble. He was asked by my mother to pay whatever was
necessary to secure the horse, but at the sale itself balked at the idea of
matching bids which pushed the selling price way beyond what he considered reasonable and so made no bid. Vaguely Noble was sold for 136,000
guineas and went on to beat Sir Ivor in the 1968 Prix de l'Arc de Triomphe
before being sold as a stallion at a valuation of £2 million.

'I'm surprised Sol Moratalla still speaks to me,' wrote Peter after
recounting this episode in his autobiography; but she does, and we have
been partners in several horses. The first was Lady Attiva, a cousin of
Attivo trained by Pat Rohan, and the best has been Amigos, who won on
the Flat and over hurdles before breaking down in his first race over fences.

It was through Peter that I was introduced to Jimmy FitzGerald, who has
trained for me such fine horses as Sapience, Sybillin and Trainglot, and
despite that little problem over Vaguely Noble, I always consult Peter
before buying or selling a horse and invariably follow his advice.

If racing isn't fun there's no point in it, and over many years Peter has
increased my fun enormously. I've always admired him – he's the best
commentator in the world – but much more important, he's the best friend
I've ever had.

Sir John Sparrow, Chairman of the Horserace Betting Levy Board, has particular memories of Peter O'Sullevan.

Sir John Sparrow

When Ian Trethowan telephoned me in 1985 and asked me to chair a small committee looking at the future of the National Stud, he opened the first of a number of doors which have successively increased my involvement in British horse racing and with the many people who contribute to that great sport. Ian told me that one member of the committee would be Peter O'Sullevan. At that time, although a committed racegoer, I knew no more of Peter than his success as a journalist with the *Daily Express*, his ownership of Attivo, and his pre-eminence as a television commentator on my favourite sport. His beguiling skills as an auctioneer, and his unstinting efforts for equine charities, had yet to be revealed to me.

In the course of the committee's work, and in the light of Peter's contribution, I learned to value the sound judgement and quiet dispassion which he added to his encyclopaedic knowledge of our subject-matter. We also became firm friends, a state of affairs which I am happy to say has continued to this day and which I very much hope will continue for many years to come.

While the committee was still sitting, I was invited to climb to the top of the old Members' Stand at Newbury to watch Peter commentating on a race. This was meant to be a treat for my infant granddaughters, but I suspect that I enjoyed it even more than they did. Among other things, it gave me the opportunity to recognize the remarkable aura of calmness which envelops Peter when he is working, in a world in which everything is frenetic activity. It was only later, when we had discovered by chance that he and Pat have the same taste in hotels as my wife and I, that I came to understand just how much hard work has to go into the preparation of those flawless commentaries. If genius is in fact 1 per cent inspiration and 99 per cent perspiration, then Peter's unvarying habit of going off to his hotel room after dinner, not to rest but to do his homework for the next day's racing, amply justifies 99 per cent of the description. Anyone who has heard one of his commentaries will be able to speak for the 1 per cent.

It was on a train from Liverpool, following a Grand National two or three years ago, that Peter told me that he hoped he would be able to get to his fiftieth Grand National commentary in 1997 before he retired. It is a great delight to all his admirers that he has achieved that ambition and it is a comfort to Cynthia and me to know that we can hope to bump into Peter and Pat – and Silva the poodle – at one or other of the hotels at which we have, without any prior planning, so frequently found ourselves in residence together. He will long be remembered in racing as a great commentator, but he is more than that: he is one of racing's great gentlemen.

Sir John ('Jakie') Astor has owned many fine racehorses, often called to their greatest triumphs by Peter O'Sullevan.

Sir John Astor

I have known Peter O'Sullevan for over fifty years and have watched him become the generally accepted voice of racing. The impression that he always leaves with me is of a man who is totally bound up with his job and is meticulously careful to be accurate and thoroughly professional.

Peter's interests in racing are broad-based and many-sided. He is sentimental about horses, and the work he has put into seeing that horses are not exploited by people is legendary. It has been typical of Peter that he should be associated with making the Grand National a safer and fairer race. Apart from his knowledge of horses, he is conversant with every aspect of betting and as a tipster he is second to none.

Peter has always been very much his own man, and his election to membership of the Jockey Club was widely applauded as a deserved tribute. There is no better company than Peter. I can only hope that his talents will continue to be used in some form or other.

One admirer came to racing late in life ...

Marion Johnson

I am a comparative newcomer to this sport that Peter O'Sullevan has graced for so many years. At sixty-seven years of age, seven months widowed, my entire knowledge of horse racing was three names: the Derby, Lester Piggott, and the Grand National; I'd also heard of Peter O'Sullevan, but did not know what he did. Then, in the winter of 1991–2, through a Dick Francis book and a Saturday afternoon in front of the television, I 'found' the National Hunt variety, and I was hooked. From then on, I watched as often as I could, read books about it, sat enthralled through the Cheltenham Festival, and eagerly awaited Aintree.

The Grand National was all that I had anticipated, and more. The lead-up to it, the profiles of the horses, trainers and riders so helpful and comprehensive, though I didn't understand all the terms, and the race itself – tremendous. How did the commentators remember all the horses? Even with the jockeys' colours in the newspaper, I was lost. The last two fences, and the run-in, as Peter talked us through them, found me on the edge of my chair, thumping my knees, and shouting, 'Come on Carl! Come on!'

This should, of course, have made me an instant admirer of Peter O'Sullevan. No such thing. It made me instead a lasting fan of Party Politics, Carl Llewellyn and Nick Gaselee, the trainer, so that, learning of an open day at Lambourn, I went with the express purpose of seeing at least one of them, and actually met and talked to all three of them. I told Mr Gaselee how I was so carried away that, sitting by myself, I was shouting for them. He said, 'Yes, Peter O'Sullevan is an excellent commentator.' It stopped me dead. That was it. That's what did it. With him calling the horses, you were there, in the crowd. You were almost on the horse, willing it to win, urging it on. From then on I listened with my head as well as my heart to all the commentators. Their reading of a race, and comments, have helped me enjoy racing so much more; but Peter, as I think everyone will agree, is the very best.

In 1993, having by then been to race meetings, and being a little more knowledgeable, I waited and hoped that Party Politics could do it again. How sad it was for all concerned. The hold-ups at the beginning, the two false starts, John White's devastation, and poor Keith Brown. Through it all, Peter's professionalism shone through. No accusations, no suppositions, no guesses or hasty words. Just the facts, presented in a calm, orderly fashion. The supreme commentator. How I admired him then.

What joy, though, since to hear him as I first remember him, calling home subsequent National winners: Miinnehoma, Royal Athlete, Rough Quest . . . and who next?

No one, they say, is indispensable, but many are sorely missed. One of these will surely be Peter O'Sullevan.

Sir Thomas Pilkington is Senior Steward of the Jockey Club, of which Peter O'Sullevan is one of the very few journalists to have been elected a member.

Sir Thomas Pilkington

Peter was elected a member of the Jockey Club in December 1986, by which time I'd known him for some thirty years, having first met him – at a Manchester dog track! – through Clive Graham, whom I knew well before I knew Peter.

Since his election, Peter has been very active at our regular meetings, dispensing the extraordinary depth of experience which makes him such a valuable member. His greatest asset is that he is totally unafraid to make his views felt, and although he may not be a great one for committees, he has been a vocal and influential presence.

His particular zeal has been directed to the cause of horse welfare, and he has been a major advocate for improving regulations concerning the use of the whip. But he has also been the voice of enthusiasm, and has inspired everybody – from Bert at the garage to the most senior members of the Jockey Club – with that enthusiasm.

Owner and breeder Bob McCreery is another old friend and long-standing admirer.

Bob McCreery

No one has ever done more for the horse in racing than Peter. Through his tireless charity work and his general concern for horse welfare, he has raised awareness of the necessity for looking after the interests of the horse.

He has been, of course, a great racing journalist, and for me a measure of his importance was the role he played at the time of the notorious Hill House affair in 1967. Hill House, trained by Ryan Price, won the Schweppes Gold Trophy at Newbury (now the Tote Gold Trophy) under circumstances which led some to believe that the horse had not been running on his merits on his outings immediately before that race. After Hill House's victory in the Schweppes a storm broke over Ryan Price's head, and racing got itself into a real tizz when it was subsequently discovered that Hill House's post-race specimen had proved positive to a banned substance. The one journalist whom Ryan Price desperately wanted on his side was Peter (who was abroad at the time of the race itself): Ryan sensed that Peter would know perfectly well that he would never do anything bad to one of his horses – and indeed, once Peter had returned and injected some reason into the case, calm was restored. It later came out that Hill House was manufacturing the prohibited cortisol within his own body and Ryan Price was vindicated, but the regard in which the trainer held the O'Sullevan opinion was a mark of Peter's standing among racing professionals.

Trainer Peter Walwyn, who in 1975 sent out Grundy to win 'The Race of the Century' against Bustino, pays his own tribute.

Peter Walwyn

Peter O'Sullevan's three unfailing characteristics throughout his long and distinguished career have been his knowledge of racing; his memory; and his general enthusiasm for the game.

As a commentator, his delivery is superb, quite unparalleled, and his command of the English language is marvellous. As a man he is marked by his courtesy, his industry, and the way he enjoys life to the full. In some ways a very private individual, Peter can be great company, especially when decent food and wine are well supplied!

He will be sorely missed.

John McCririck, a different mould of broadcaster on Channel Four Racing, pays homage to the qualities behind 'The Voice'.

John McCririck

Peter O'Sullevan has always been the quiet professional. Nothing interferes with the meticulous, painstaking preparation essential towards making each and every calling of horses work. The rest of us burble away hopelessly in the shadow of a national landmark – assuredly soon to be Sir Peter or, if merit truly counts, Lord O'Sullevan of the Hoof.

Yet away from the microphone there's another equally dedicated side to this shy but steely character. In the steamy jungle of the betting ring he prowls alone: one of the shrewdest, best informed investors around, yet one who goes about his business, for himself and a few trusted friends and insiders, in such an unobtrusive way you hardly know he's there. Amid all the shouting and pandemonium he strikes unheralded, invariably at over the returned odds, and so often with deadly effect. And when O'Sullevan takes an ante-post price one thing is certain: that animal will be sent off far shorter!

Peter, a natural gentleman, embodies all the class of his American contemporary, that ace doyen of racing writers, Joe Hirsch – universally revered, known by everyone involved in the sport he loves from the Yank equivalents of Bert at the garage to royalty. All regard Joe as their personal friend. So with Peter, who has been a gentle guide through some of our most unforgettable moments, as archivists in centuries to come will continue to discover.

May he relish a happy retirement. He's still picking off those bookie chappies while continuing to work unsung for horse and human charities that have benefited so much down the decades from his compassion and decency.

Along with countless millions, I've grown up to regard Peter O'Sullevan as my friend too.

One of the best-known public faces among 'those bookie chappies' is Graham Sharpe, public relations front-man for William Hill and a prolific author of racing books.

Graham Sharpe

Over the years I have witnessed many people placing bets with William Hill. I have never noticed any punter's bets being treated with more respect than Peter's – a tribute, definitely, to his acknowledged judgement of horseflesh and, probably, to the many sources of information upon which he can call!

Actor James Bolam and actress Susan Jameson owned Credo's Daughter, the popular and game little mare who during the 1970s was a regular sight in the big staying chases.

James Bolam

I always think of Peter O'Sullevan as Mr Racing – a man of great knowledge about the sport but one with the knack of making it accessible to those outside. A class act himself, he makes racing classless, appealing to everybody.

Most of the big races in which Credo's Daughter ran in the mid-1970s were covered by the BBC, and watching the recordings always brings back to me what a superlative commentator Peter has been. It seemed to me that he tended to prefer those stout-hearted old chasers who are seen out year after year – like our mare – to the flash-in-the-pan Flat types, and it also struck me that you could detect when he had a certain fondness for a particular horse. When he abbreviated our mare's name to 'Credo's', that for me was a sure sign of his affection for her.

One day she was disqualified after passing the post first in a chase at Newbury – after jumping the last, she'd had to move out to go round the water jump, and was adjudged to have pushed the other horse out the way (though she was such a little thing, how could she have shoved anything out the way?). We were miffed by this decision, and although he was far too correct to say that he felt she'd been hard done by, the little twinkle in his eye when he spoke to Sue and me after the race left me in little doubt where his sympathies lay!

His retirement marks the end of an era. A man with great charisma, great warmth and great style – to use that word again, class.

And from a letter from a viewer in Rochestown, County Cork . . .

Rory Burke

I am writing just to let you know how much pleasure you have brought to me over the years. I am a big racing fan and racing to me is not the same when Peter O'Sullevan is not calling the race.

I am twenty-nine years old and have been going racing ever since I could walk. Every Sunday from New Year's Day to the last Sunday in May I go to the point-to-point races in the Cork, Waterford and Kerry areas. We have had many point-to-point horses over the years, and last year we had a nice gelding by Carlingford Castle which was named Four From Home. I got this name from your race commentary – thank you – and now this horse is trained by the great Jonjo O'Neill.

I understand that you will hang up your 'mike' in the coming year. Do you really have to? I will miss your velvet voice on the telly: you are the best horse racing commentator in the history of live broadcasting and the best reader of the game. Your love of horses shines through every broadcast, with over fifty years' involvement in the Sport of Kings.

No one ever will replace you. In fact no one should be allowed to.

I wish you the best for the future. I hope you will be around for a long time to come so that maybe some day I might meet you at some race meeting.

The BBC's racing broadcasts will never be the same again.

Peter – please change your mind.

10

The great commentaries

– and the homework behind them

TELEVISION (Talks)

THE BRITISH BROADCASTING CORPORATION

Broadcasting House, London, W.I

TELEPHONE : WELBECK 4468   TELEGRAMS : BROADCASTS, TELEX, LONDON

Our Reference : 03/PC/CG

January 13th, 1948

DEAR

We invite you to prepare and broadcast a talk(s) in our television programmes as detailed below upon the conditions printed overleaf. If you accept, kindly sign and return the attached confirmation sheet, or reply otherwise, as soon as possible. (See condition 1 overleaf.)

Title.................Kempton Park Racing..............

Date(s) : Rehearsal(s) ....January 31st.............   Broadcast....January 31st....

Time : Rehearsal(s) Time as arranged with Mr............   Broadcast....   (a) 1.50. – 2.10.p.m.   2.0
Peter Dimmock   (b) 2.20. – 2.40.p.m.   2.30
Place Kempton Park.lace   (c) 2.55. – 3.05.p.m.   3.0

Fee .Fifteen guineas (£15.15.0.) including expenses. To commentate as discussed
                                                    with Mr. Peter Dimmock.

Letters addressed to speakers c/o the BBC will be forwarded, but for statistical purposes the letters may be opened before being forwarded unless we are notified of any objection. Letters marked "Personal" are forwarded unopened.

Producer: Mr. Peter Dimmock
Tel: Tudor 6420.

Yours faithfully,

THE BRITISH BROADCASTING CORPORATION

Holland Bennett

Programme Contracts Department

Peter O'Sullevan Esq.,
14, Beverley Houses,
Britten Street,
S.W.3.

P/412/P 6-6-47 3000 SM

Many of the contributors to this book have remarked how Peter O'Sullevan's commentaries have formed an inseparable part of racing's collective memory of the great races. You cannot think of Red Rum's third Grand National or Dawn Run's Gold Cup without hearing the libretto of those well-remembered and familiar phrases. For those honing their Peter O'Sullevan impressions, but primarily for those who simply want a record of the great callings, here are transcripts of six of the O'Sullevan best – plus, at the end of this section, a behind-the-scenes look at how he does his homework.

Cheltenham Gold Cup, 7 March 1964

Just four runners for the 1964 Cheltenham Gold Cup, but this was one of the most keenly anticipated races since the war, with Mill House, winner of the Gold Cup in 1963 and widely thought – at least in England, where he was trained by Fulke Walwyn – to be invincible, taking on Arkle, trained in Ireland by Tom Dreaper. Arkle had finished third to Mill House in the previous November's Hennessy Gold Cup but his supporters knew he had slipped badly after landing over the third last fence. They were confident of revenge in the Gold Cup, while the Mill House camp would not hear of defeat. The two outsiders, King's Nephew and 1960 Gold Cup winner Pas Seul, were beaten off as Mill House and Arkle reached the top of the hill on the second circuit.

. . . And it's the big two now as they run down the hill to the third last fence. The big horse, Mill House, with Arkle closing on him. And it's Mill House and Willie Robinson, Arkle and Pat Taaffe, and Pat being shouted for from the stands now. Irish voices really beginning to call for him now as he starts to make up ground on Arkle. It's Mill House the leader from Arkle. Arkle making ground on the far side at the third last fence. Mill House is over the leader from Arkle second. They've got two fences left to jump now in the Gold Cup, with Mill House the leader from Arkle and a long way back is Pas Seul, then King's Nephew. This is the second last fence and they're still both full of running, still going great guns – both of them. It's Mill House on the inside jumps it only just ahead of Arkle. Now they're rounding the home turn and this is it! And Willie Robinson's got his whip out and Pat Taaffe is shaking up Arkle and this is the race now to the last fence! It's Arkle on the stands side for Ireland and Mill House for England on the far side. And this is it with Arkle just taking the lead as they come to the last fence. It's gonna be Arkle if he jumps it. Arkle coming to the last now and Arkle a length clear of Mill House. He's over and clear. Mill House is trying to challenge him again but it's Arkle on the stands side, Mill House over on the far side. Coming up towards the line and Arkle is holding him. Arkle going away now from Mill House. This is the champion! This is the best we've seen for a long time. Arkle is the winner of the Gold Cup. Mill House is second . . .

Vernons November Sprint Cup, 5 November 1966

The inaugural running of the Vernons November Sprint Cup in 1966 saw Peter O'Sullevan on the brink of his biggest victory as an owner, in what was at the time the richest all-aged sprint ever run in England. Be Friendly was one of five two-year-olds in a field of fifteen runners, and started at 15–2 third favourite behind Lucasland and Dondeen.

They're off and the first to show is Kamundu, a very fast break towards the outside. And it's Kamundu from Potier as they race towards the bend with Green Park going up on the outside of Kamundu. And it's the two-year-old Green Park now with Be Friendly moving up into second place. Be Friendly and Green Park, the two youngsters, disputing it and coming right across to the stands side. Over on the far side it's Spanish Sail. In the centre of the course Kamundu running very fast. Go Shell right up there with them and also Dondeen. And it's Dondeen and Go Shell disputing it now from Spanish Sail. Right under the stands rail – it's difficult to know how you relate to those on the far side – is Be Friendly with Green Park. On the far side Go Shell just leads Spanish Sail, then comes Hard Man. Dondeen still in the centre of the course being pressed now by the favourite Lucasland. And Dondeen the grey now from Lucasland, then comes Forlorn River. And on the stands side it's Be Friendly from Green Park. And it's Be Friendly and Green Park on the stands side, Dondeen in the centre. Be Friendly just the leader now from Green Park in second place. Then comes Dondeen. They're racing up towards the line and Be Friendly is the leader from Green Park and Dondeen. Be Friendly going away from Green Park and Dondeen. And at the line it's Be Friendly the winner, Green Park is second, Dondeen is third. That's the result. It's a photo for fourth place between Potier, Polistina and Forlorn River. But no doubt about the winner, and the official result of the Vernons November Sprint Cup: first number 13, Be Friendly, owned by [*brief pause, then dismissively:*] Peter O'Sullevan, trained by Cyril Mitchell and ridden by Colin Williams, second number 11, Green Park . . .

King George VI and Queen Elizabeth Diamond Stakes, 26 July 1975

This famous clash of the generations between 1974 St Leger winner Bustino and 1975 Derby winner Grundy, with the supporting cast led by the great French mare Dahlia, who in 1973 and 1974 had become the first horse ever to win the King George twice, produced a titanic struggle which immediately brought the race the epithet it has borne since: The Race of the Century.

. . . And they're past the half-mile marker now and racing towards the home turn and it's Bustino who's gone on from Grundy! And it's Bustino now in the lead from Grundy the favourite in second, then comes Star Appeal third, Dahlia's coming there strongly four, behind Dahlia is Ashmore, then Libra's Rib and Card King as they level up for home. And Bustino from Grundy in second, Star Appeal and Dahlia, then Ashmore, then On My Way beginning a run towards the stands side at the two-furlong marker. And it's Bustino, Joe Mercer, being pressed by Pat Eddery now, Grundy, then Dahlia in third place as they race towards the furlong pole! It's Bustino and Grundy together, then comes Dahlia, then On My Way! Bustino on the far side, Grundy on the near side, the three-year-old and the four-year-old as they race into the final hundred and fifty yards. And it's Grundy going on from Bustino and Dahlia and On My Way. Bustino's fighting his way back but Grundy's holding him and as they come to the line – Grundy wins it, Bustino is second, Dahlia third . . .

News of the World Grand National, 2 April 1977

Red Rum had won the Grand National in 1973, catching the gallant front-running Crisp in the shadow of the winning post, and followed up with an easy victory in the 1974 race. In both the following years Red Rum finished runner-up – to L'Escargot in 1975 and to Rag Trade in 1976 – and in 1977, even at the advanced age of twelve, this Aintree specialist was poised to become the first ever triple Grand National winner as commentator John Hanmer, having brought the horses back across the Melling Road on the second circuit, called 'Over to you, Peter ...'

... And it's Red Rum, with two loose horses around him now, just two fences left to jump between he and Grand National history. But close in behind him is Churchtown Boy. The Pilgarlic is about six lengths away, then comes the mare Eyecatcher and then What A Buck and behind them Happy Ranger then Forest King and Carroll Street. They're virtually the only ones left in the 1977 Grand National, and Churchtown Boy is still making relentless progress, Martin Blackshaw coming there very sweetly on Churchtown Boy. But Red Rum – he's still holding the lead now as they jump the second last. He's over the second last in the lead. Churchtown Boy didn't jump it too well. And it's Red Rum and Tommy Stack now from Churchtown Boy, The Pilgarlic and Eyecatcher as they come to the last fence in the National. And Red Rum with a tremendous chance of winning his third National! He jumps it clear of Churchtown Boy. He's getting the most tremendous cheer from the crowd: they're willing him home now, the twelve-year-old Red Rum, being preceded only by loose horses, being chased by Churchtown Boy, Eyecatcher has moved into third, The Pilgarlic fourth. They're coming to the Elbow. There's a furlong now between Red Rum and his third Grand National triumph. And he's coming up to the line, to win it like a fresh horse in great style. It's hats off and a tremendous reception – you've never heard one like it at Liverpool! Red Rum wins the National! ...

Tote Cheltenham Gold Cup, 13 March 1986

If Red Rum's 1977 National represented a moment unique in racing history, so did Dawn Run's Cheltenham Gold Cup in 1986. The Irish mare had won the Champion Hurdle in 1984 and was now favourite to become the first horse ever to win Champion Hurdle and Gold Cup.

. . . Now there are just two fences left to jump in the Gold Cup, and it's Run And Skip, over on the far side the mare Dawn Run, Wayward Lad the veteran on the near side, and Forgive'N Forget still running very very strongly indeed, last year's winner. As they approach the second last fence – Run And Skip, Dawn Run, Wayward Lad and Forgive'N Forget coming there strongly on the stands side. At the second last, Run And Skip, Dawn Run, Wayward Lad, Forgive'N Forget still coming there strongly on the near side. Forgive'N Forget on the near side now as they come to the final fence. Forgive'N Forget is going to jump marginally in the lead from Wayward Lad. Forgive'N Forget on the near side, Wayward Lad on the far side. It's Wayward Lad, the veteran, trying to break his Cheltenham hoodoo, being pressed now by Dawn Run in the centre. Forgive'N Forget on the near side. As they race to the line, and the mare's beginning to get up! And as they come to the line, she's made it! Dawn Run has won it! Dawn Run has won it from Wayward Lad. And Jonjo O'Neill punches the air as the mare has made Turf history here at Cheltenham: she's become the first in history to win the Champion Hurdle and the Gold Cup . . .

Tote Cheltenham Gold Cup, 16 March 1989

With his bold front-running style and flamboyant jumping, the grey Desert Orchid had made himself the most popular horse in years. But Cheltenham had never been his ideal course, and at the last minute the weather had appeared to ruin the horse's chance of winning the Gold Cup. In going much heavier than he liked, Desert Orchid had it all to do rounding the final bend . . .

. . . It's Desert Orchid now as they race to the home turn, from Yahoo, chasing him all the time and trying to get up on the inside, with Charter Party third. Desert Orchid and Yahoo now as they race round the home turn, with very little between them. Yahoo on the far side – he's gone on now from Desert Orchid towards the near side. Yahoo from Desert Orchid, and Desert Orchid looks as though he's tiring in the ground! Yahoo who loves the mud is full of running at the second last. Yahoo jumps from Desert Orchid, but Desert Orchid is rallying, he's trying to come again towards the near side. It's Yahoo on the far side, Desert Orchid towards the near side. Desert Orchid's accelerating as they come to the last. Yahoo on the far side, Desert Orchid on the near side. It's Desert Orchid on the near side, Yahoo on the far side – Desert Orchid drifting over towards the stands side. He's beginning to get up! Desert Orchid is beginning to get up as they race towards the line! There's a tremendous cheer from the crowd, as Desert Orchid is going to win it! Desert Orchid has won the Gold Cup, Yahoo is second, third is Charter Party . . .

★

The homework

Every Peter O'Sullevan race commentary is preceded by hours of preparation – familiarizing himself with riders' colours, with the distinctive markings of each horse, with details of the jockeys and trainers, and with appropriate facts and figures.

In the centre spread of the section of colour photographs in this book (between pages 96 and 97) is reproduced the chart which he prepared before calling the 1996 Martell Grand National by pasting on to a large cardboard folder the entry for each runner from a proof of the racecard, then colouring in the outline of each jockey on stickers and placing these alongside each entry.

At the top of the chart are written the numbers of the most significant fences (the first open ditch is 3, Becher's Brook 6 and 22, the Canal Turn 8 and 24, Valentine's Brook 9 and 25, the Chair 15, the water jump 16, the final fence 30), along with various useful facts: 1996 sees the thirty-seventh televised Grand National (yes, the void 1993 race does count!); Grittar in 1982 was the last winning favourite; Sergeant Murphy in 1923 the last thirteen-year-old to win; there are seven jockeys riding in the race for the first time; the runners have won 221 races between them; and so on.

Horse number 1, Young Hustler, is ridden by 27-year-old Chris Maude, having his second ride in the race. This is Young Hustler's third attempt at the National, and he has won fifteen of his fifty-eight races.

That horse number 2, Life Of A Lord, is trained in Ireland is indicated by his name being highlighted in green rather than yellow. Life Of A Lord has won the Kerry National, and will miss the race if the going is soft, according to trainer Aidan O'Brien.

Deep Bramble (3) wears a sheepskin noseband ('SNB'). Son Of War (4), also trained in Ireland and winner of the Jameson Irish Grand National in 1994, is the first National runner for his trainer Peter McCreery; the last grey to win the Grand National was in 1961, thirty-five years ago.

Carl Llewellyn, rider of Party Politics (6), won the National on that horse in 1992; Party Politics was also second in 1995. Richard Dunwoody on number 9, Superior Finish, won it in 1986 and 1994 – and his mount is running in the name of Peter McGrane as the prize in a competition in *The Sun* newspaper.

The circles round the numbers 15, 18, 19 and 26 indicate that those horses are wearing blinkers or a visor. Number 16, Bavard Dieu, is a chestnut with two white socks on his hind legs and a white blaze on his face. Frank Woods, rider of number 13, Wylde Hide (who was the first horse to win the Thyestes Chase twice), is the son of Paddy Woods, who won the Irish Grand National twice and also won over hurdles on Arkle. David Walsh, rider of number 15, Riverside Boy, is the youngest rider in the race: the asterisk by his name shows that this is his first National ride. Over The Deel (20), third in the race in 1995, was the prize in a competition organized by Littlewoods and won by David Davies, nineteen years old and unemployed. Three Brownies (26) is a three-parts brother to Lastofthebrownies, fourth in the Grand National in 1989.

'X1' against Superior Finish, Bishops Hall, Bavard Dieu, Vicompt de Valmont and Sure Metal indicates that those horses are carrying one pound overweight.

Plastic Spaceage (number 24) misses the race on account of a bruised foot.

Study that chart and you'll pick up enough information to try it for yourself. So get out the video of the 1996 Martell Grand National, find the place where the starter climbs up on to his rostrum, turn down the sound – and it's over to you . . .

Acknowledgements

The editor and publishers are grateful to Express Newspapers for the use of three cartoons by Giles, and to Mirror Group Newspapers for the use of the cartoon by David Langdon. The John Skeaping drawing of horses and jockeys is from a private collection.

They are also very grateful to:

the *Daily Mail* for the piece by Peter Scudamore;

the *Daily Telegraph* for the extract from the piece by Russell Davies;

Mainstream Publishing for the adapted extract from *Die Broke* by Jamie Reid;

The Observer for the piece by Hugh McIlvanney;

the *Radio Times* for the piece by Clement Freud;

the *Racing Post* for the piece by John Oaksey;

the *Sporting Life* for the extract from the piece by Chris McGrath and for the piece by Ian Carnaby;

Timeform for the extract from the entry on Attivo in *Chasers & Hurdlers 1975–76*;

The Times for the extract from the piece by Henry Kelly;

. . . and to all those who have agreed for their letters to Peter O'Sullevan to be quoted.

The editor wishes to express his personal thanks to the Rapid Reaction Force – Gillian Bromley (heroine yet again) and Charlie Webster.

HOORAY for Peter O'Sullevan! He landed his sixth nap in a row at Liverpool yesterday.

HOORAY for Peter O'Sullevan! He gave a 25—1 hat-trick yesterday for the second time this week.

Pet Ev giv sta ha fra

EXPRESS SATURDAY NOVEMBER 5 1966

Raving mad? Well let's Be Friendly

By PETER O'SULLEVAN

YDOCK'S 15-runner Vernons November Sprint Cup, eaturing winners of 57 races, is the richest all-age t ever staged in Britain.

he winner will collect £5,387 5s., second £653, 3rd 10s., 4th £163 5s.

nd if you think your correspondent is raving mad to ose No. 13 Be Friendly (2.30 nap) you are in good any.

Cousins, responsible for 5 Ayr Gold Cup winner and ear's W. D. and H. O. Wills n first, Kamundu, affirmed ve to one against any of ve two-year-olds beating the ns."

en Park's trainer Jeremy has "an even £50" that his r of the £7,550 Cornwallis beats Be Friendly. And y Lindley, who has ridden youngsters, declares he "has no earthly chance ver with Green Park."

eform rated 'Lucasland. r of York's Senior Service. arket's July Cup and Ascot's m. 18lb. superior to Be dly at the weights. And s Be Friendly to finish ninth. mindex places us eighth d Lucasland and Dondeen orlorn River.

himself showed no signs scouragement when accept-ugar from me in the race-s stables yesterday.

Supporter

r did his 'lad" Tony Boyle received The Racehorse y certificate of merit for the immaculately turned out when "his" colt last red at Newbury.

We have another supporter in my long time friend "Quinnie" Gilbey, 21-years-old Kettledrum of the Sporting Chronicle.

He announced in the Press room at Haydock yesterday: "I am going for Be Friendly. And what is more he will win.

Mind you Quinnie can afford to be confident. One of the best racing journalists in the history of the game is writing his last column today.

So he won't be around if the need arises to apologise to aggrieved readers.

To carry madness to a point of insanity I am naming Be Friendly to win from Green Park and Kamundu.

What about the "hot pot" Lucasland? At her best she is a "moral" and owner John Baillie's confidence is reflected in the fact that around a fortnight ago he insured against the race being abandoned through adverse weather.

Whatever the outcome none would grudge success to Lucas-land's most ardent pursuer, Don-deen, twice a winner under big weights this season.

At Sandown I am hoping Freddie (2.25) will profit from Arkle's absence from the Gallaher Gold Cup.

Red Rum it again—M

By Peter O'S

RED RUM has a favourite's chance to win the National yet again on Saturday, April 2.

That is the inevitable reaction following publication of the weights.

For the little old local hero and Aintree regular, who carries his years (12) so lightly, has 11st. 8lb.

This is the lightest burden he has been set to carry, since his first triumph under 10st. 5lb. in 1973.

Since then, "Rummy" has won under 12st. and finished runner-up from both the same handicap mark and with 11st. 10lb.

Not surprisingly, "Ginger" McCain is confirmed in his belief that the legend of

Southport Sands can make history by winning the world's greatest steeplechase for the third time.

"He's in super shape after his winter holiday and work-ing really well." says the handler of Noel Le Mare's hero.

The Tote is out-betting leading bookmakers by nam-ing Red Rum the 14—1 ante-post favourite. Hills, Lad-brokes and Mecca are all two points shorter, while Corals offer no more than 10—1.

The "American" Fort Devon predictably heads the handicap with 12 stone. The Gold Cup has prior con-sideration in his curriculum, but the detail that he will be left in until a late stage

befo final being

Fr week (1st. Nati Cha diate

At neigh 8lb.). Fort and (sta and trea

Si obse pron dav pick

Fr

O'Sullevan gives 181-1

PETER O'SULLEVAN leads the I've-Got-A-Horse (and it won) Parade this morning with a smashing 181—1 treble.

O'Sullevan gives only three tips each day. Yesterday's trio were all winners. Here they are :—

NOORANI (nap)	7—1
APPROVAL	6—1
NOBLE CHARGER	9—4

Newmarket Correspondent also gave Noorani an Airmark (6—), while Sir Harry, the Northern C three winners at Haydock . . . all of which is part of th

Followers also in the mo fine winners at

BALLYLINA CLOYNE ....

as well as thr other three at two non-runner

TRICOTINE

'Sullevan's III-I double

TER O'SULLEVAN came up trumps again on urday, when he completed the Autumn Double with n Cherry (13—2) in the Cesarewitch. A fortnight ago successfully named Intermission (14—1) for the leg, the Cambridgeshire. The double odds—a ulous 111—1. Today's Racing : Page 18

Daily Express Racing Se

's Arkle for Pat's | birthday | present

12/3/63